TAPESTRY
A Loving Weave of Living, Dying, and Spirit

Judith Elizabeth Bowen

ARS METAPHYSICA

an imprint of Sunbury Press, Inc.
Mechanicsburg, PA USA

an imprint of Sunbury Press, Inc.
Mechanicsburg, PA USA

Copyright © 2020 by Judith Elizabeth Bowen.
Cover Copyright © 2020 by Sunbury Press, Inc.

Sunbury Press supports copyright. Copyright fuels creativity, encourages diverse voices, promotes free speech, and creates a vibrant culture. Thank you for buying an authorized edition of this book and for complying with copyright laws. Except for the quotation of short passages for the purpose of criticism and review, no part of this publication may be reproduced, scanned, or distributed in any form without permission. You are supporting writers and allowing Sunbury Press to continue to publish books for every reader. For information contact Sunbury Press, Inc., Subsidiary Rights Dept., PO Box 548, Boiling Springs, PA 17007 USA or legal@sunburypress.com.

For information about special discounts for bulk purchases, please contact Sunbury Press Orders Dept. at (855) 338-8359 or orders@sunburypress.com.

To request one of our authors for speaking engagements or book signings, please contact Sunbury Press Publicity Dept. at publicity@sunburypress.com.

FIRST ARS METAPHYSICA EDITION: July 2020

Set in Adobe Garamond | Interior design by Crystal Devine | Cover design by Lawrence Knorr | Edited by Jennifer Cappello.

Publisher's Cataloging-in-Publication Data
Names: Bowen, Judith Elizabeth, author.
Title: Tapestry : a loving weave of living, dying, and spirit / Judith Elizabeth Bowen.
Description: First trade paperback edition. | Mechanicsburg, PA : Ars Metaphysica, 2020.
Summary: A journey through the heart, leading to the vulnerability that allows compassion and healing for oneself, as well as the other.
Identifiers: ISBN: 978-1-620063-71-2 (softcover).
Subjects: BIOGRAPHY & AUTOBIOGRAPHY / Personal Memoirs | FAMILY & RELATIONSHIPS / Marriage & Long-Term Relationships | FAMILY & RELATIONSHIPS / Death, Grief, Bereavement.

Product of the United States of America
0 1 1 2 3 5 8 13 21 34 55

Continue the Enlightenment!

For Mary and Katharine

For Mark and Michelle

and for
all those who wound themselves into our lives.

Contents

CHAPTERS

1.	The Question	1
2.	In the Beginning	3
3.	New Love and New Realities	11
4.	Rock Formation	26
5.	A Glimmer of New Perspectives	44
6.	A Healing Path	58
7.	All Was Not as We Had Dreamed	76
8.	Turning Point	100
9.	New Directions	121
10.	Caretaker for the Duration	142
11.	The Ending	165
12.	Fly Away	192
13.	Epilogue	199
	Notes	203
	Acknowledgments	204
	About the Author	206

CHAPTER 1

THE QUESTION

When did it all begin—this slow decline? The question tugs at me as the scent of citrus blossoms drifts gently through the windows of the place I call my healing room. Curtains lift with the soft breeze, and I wonder: Was it four years ago? That's when I came here to the relaxed pace of this small Texas town in the Rio Grande Valley, to take a new and challenging position. Or did it begin two years ago? That's when my husband and I came together again after our jobs kept us separate, me in Texas and him in Kentucky. Or was it as long ago as the time of the first cancer? That was when we moved to Lexington, a lifetime ago. Was it sometime before or in between? I reach for my journal—my private place of escape—trying to understand, to find the beginning point, and I start writing.

I arrived here filled with excitement. I came to Edinburg, Texas, on my own and with all of my dreams, to take a new position in March 1996. I loved the challenge, the adventure of it. I did well. But it left us apart for two years; not what we planned.

Two years of searching yielded no path that would allow my husband to join me. He received five rejections, neither one of us understanding the why of it until hindsight allowed.

I knew he had faced health difficulties in those two years. I had loved him through the healing, across the miles.

One day Earle announced, "I can't do this anymore. I am eligible for early retirement, and I just need to be with you."

He came, then, to Texas, with his dreams and fantasies of what retirement would be like, dreams spun with a gossamer web. And so, we came back together.

CHAPTER 2

In the Beginning

Dr. T. Earle Bowen. The name was at the top of the syllabus for the Health Care Administration III class required for the master's in public administration program at Memphis State University. I was scanning for the room number, making sure I knew where to go, in a hurry again, preoccupied with my mental checklist. Did I complete final details at work? Did I fill in my husband about the children's dinner? He had come in the door at the last minute, as I had been about to leave, as always. Now I needed to find my classroom. It was fall of 1978, the beginning of my final year. My specialty was healthcare administration.

The pace of two evening classes a week for the past year had become familiar. I loved the excitement of new learning. It was the engine that powered me through the coursework. I finally found the classroom, grateful for a chance to sit after running up the stairs. The hum of the fluorescent lights matched the hum of blood in my ears as I found a seat in the middle of the room. Many students were already in place and I allowed myself to slow down.

Health Care Administration III was described as a nuts-and-bolts course on the intricacies of institutional structure and function. The content was relevant to my work as an occupational therapist.

Dr. Bowen and a colleague were listed as the co-instructors.

Earle Bowen, as he identified himself, came striding into the classroom that first evening—a large carrying case slung over one shoulder and a briefcase in the other hand—saying, "Hi" to everyone in general. He busied himself pulling out teaching materials and setting up a slide projector. "I want this to be a fun class," he said with a marked Southern accent.

"Life is a little busy right now. I just got back from a trip to Egypt and I'm trying to reconnect with work and my kids," he chatted as he set up. His longish, wavy brown hair and well-trimmed beard, and shirtsleeves rolled up to his elbows took him a step beyond the usual academic look. Blue eyes behind large, wire-rimmed glasses seemed not to miss a thing. He asked about our backgrounds and interests and listened carefully. It was my turn.

"I'm an occupational therapist," I said. "I've worked in a number of health-care settings over the last twelve years. I most often end up feeling like I'm banging my head against a brick wall when I try to convince administrators of the value of programs I'd like to develop. I need more learning. I want to be more effective. That's why I'm here."

"We'll see if we can help you find some answers," he said. I felt as though I was seen and heard.

He made eye contact with whomever he talked to and was to the point in responding to questions. His co-instructor stood quietly to the side in seeming deference.

As Dr. Bowen talked, I thought, *He must enjoy being physically active.* He was well-muscled and moved easily. I saw right away that he had a gift for making concepts clear and reflective of the reality of institutional function. He and his colleague had worked and taught together before and had an easy back-and-forth teaching style. He was a good instructor who was also pleasant to look at. *This will make the class quite enjoyable*, I thought.

As an occupational therapist, I knew the ways a body speaks. I learned to observe what my clients told me about themselves without using words. I noticed quality of movement, skin tone, the body's ways of expressing itself as an energetic entity. I learned how the scent of a person changes with illness and how skin feels when the body is not in balance. Somewhere, I learned to see beyond what was presented on the surface and with words. Perhaps I had always had that gift.

One evening well into the semester, as I watched Earle move and interact as he taught, I suddenly felt that I was in another energetic space—removed from the class—as though I were observing it from a distance. I was in the class, but apart from it. A thought, a knowing came to me at that moment: *I am going to marry this man*. If I had to explain it, I would not connect it to anything specific that he was teaching or doing. I can only tell you that it came, most unexpectedly, from someplace in me that connected with some energy in him. I was terrified. Absolutely terrified. Each of us was married and had children. I had no idea what to do with this, and so I shut it down and tucked it away. The course ended, and I went on with my work, my life, and my learning.

In summer 1979, an independent study was required, for which I would need a mentor. I wanted to create an evaluation tool that could be used for gathering specific data for the Tennessee Occupational Therapy Association, and I thought of Earle. I knew he had the expertise and experience for developing the instrument I had in mind. In preparation for that, I called him early in the spring, knowing it would take time to begin the process. He was pleasant, said he remembered me and asked if I could wait for a few weeks to meet as he had just moved into a new position. I was able to accommodate that.

And so, the next chapter began. We met in his office to begin to develop the project. I sat across the large desk from him, taking in the room: the extensive bookshelves, assorted trophies, and awards, as well as pictures of his family. It was a solid room—wood, leather, books, light from a large window. It made a statement of position as well as allowing ease of communication. We outlined steps to be accomplished, developed a plan, and set a follow-up time.

I liked Earle's competence. He analyzed what I had brought, asked pertinent questions, and gave clear direction as to how to further develop the evaluation. This, together with his direct gaze and warm manner, made me feel seen and valued. He was secure in his area of skill.

For the second meeting, I wore a deep-blue top and skirt, which I felt good in. It was a soft, draping material, and I liked how it felt to wear it. I was aware of how I looked in it. Earle invited me to sit next to him on the large leather couch along the wall of his office. We needed to sit close to go over the work I had done on the project. As we worked, there were a number of interruptions. His secretary came in with a message and there were several phone calls he had to attend to. When it was time to leave, Earle asked, "Would you be interested in meeting next time in a park? We could bring our lunch and work uninterrupted."

"Yes, I think that would work," I said. "I'm consulting at a number of agencies in the area and could manage the time if we planned it." He took a small black notebook out of his shirt pocket, which was adorned with four pens, each a different kind, and we sorted out the time. As I left the office, he reached out to touch my shoulder.

"It was a good meeting," he said.

And so, a friendship began. We met once a week if schedules allowed, to review the progress of my plan. Memphis has a fine park system, and spring was lovely. Comfortable temperatures and the relaxed setting of sun-dappled picnic areas allowed open space to develop between us that wasn't possible in an office. Songs of birds, the scent of blossoms, and occasionally young mothers with small children playing nearby took us out of our normal lives. We ate our sandwiches at picnic tables and enjoyed each other's company. I was drawn in by his fine mind, his creativity of thought, and his sense of humor.

"Tell me about your family," Earle said one day.

"I have two daughters. My older daughter, Mary, is nine, and Katie is six. I'm very proud of both of them. They are my absolute joys. Things are difficult in other ways though. I'm struggling to sort out what is happening, or not happening, with my husband and me, and I am thinking that I may need to leave the marriage." There, it was said.

"I'm having some problems at home too. My wife and I are seeing a marriage counselor. I don't know where we'll end up. All kinds of things are bubbling up."

"How about your children?"

"Mark is the oldest. He's thirteen. He's very bright and has natural athletic ability. Michelle is eight and is just a sweetheart." And with a smile, he added, "She enjoys fixing my hair. She combs it and puts it up in rollers." He chuckled.

Over the weeks that we met, Earle talked about his job and the path his career had taken, from a faculty member at the University of Alabama to an administrator at the University of Tennessee–Memphis.

"I'm grateful for the support and encouragement I got along the way," he said. "The chancellor created opportunities for me and has been fully supportive of everything I have wanted to do. I couldn't be more fortunate."

He talked often about the people he worked with and the relationships he had built over his years in that system. "I like where I am professionally."

I shared that we had just moved to Memphis some two years before.

"Because of the ages of my girls, I've been doing consulting and part-time work with a home health agency. It gives me a lot more flexibility in getting to school events or to transport them. I'm enjoying being able to do that."

"Life does get pretty complicated with kids, doesn't it?"

"Yes, it does."

The project was finally completed. The evaluation tool was implemented, analyzed, and ready to turn in. I found I wanted more time with him but didn't see how that could happen.

"Would you like to keep meeting as our schedules allow?" He asked the question as we walked side by side across the grassy park to our cars.

"Yes. I'd like that." I noticed my heart beating faster. This was uncharted territory.

I felt a tacit acknowledgment that our enjoyment of each other had become more than professional.

If we found a table that was in deep shade, it was comfortable enough to continue lunchtime visits through the summer. One day, as we sat quietly for a minute enjoying the last of our sandwiches, Earle leaned forward, his arms on the picnic table, looked at me for a moment, then said, "On the day you came to my office in that blue dress and I touched your shoulder as you left, it felt like an electric current ran from my hand all the way up my arm and into my body. I have never had anything like that happen, ever."

I heard myself saying, "I felt very close to you that day and still do." I felt charged by that same current. The feeling excited me and scared me. I felt my face flush, and I reached out to touch him. His hand met mine and the touch felt caring, solid, and true.

But we both pulled back from that moment and returned to safer discussions.

Earle did indeed enjoy physical exercise. "I plan time for racquetball and running in my schedule. Those are lunch activities as well," he said with a smile.

He pulled out his weekly planner, the small black notebook he carried in his shirt pocket along with an ever-present array of pens that made me think of medals, all lined up.

"I like tennis, sailing, canoeing, and soccer too," he continued.

All were foreign activities to me. I saw, though, how complex and demanding his schedule was.

We talked some about our families, our Northern and Southern roots.

Then he said, as though he was speaking with the rule of law, "New Year's Day in Alabama is celebrated with hog jowl and black-eyed peas along with collard greens."

I felt my face screw up. "What in heaven's name is hog jowl? How do you eat it?"

"Well, you brown it and throw it in with the beans. Oh, it's wonderful."

This was said with much gusto and a big voice and some waving of arms. I thought, *Wow, this man has appetites*!

I answered with my own rule of law. "In southeastern Pennsylvania, the meal is pork and sauerkraut!"

He looked unimpressed. There followed a heated discussion as to which way was the right way. We didn't achieve a resolution right then.

Conversation traveled to books we'd read, our enjoyment of people, and the fascinating nature of institutions. We met in a world of creative thought.

One day in late summer, we decided to walk a bit on a path through the park. The crape myrtle still bloomed, a welcome bit of color amid the intense green of other foliage. Earle stopped under a tree so we'd have some shade and turned to me. "There is something I want to say."

I looked up at him, wondering.

"I want you to know that what is going on between my wife and me has nothing to do with you. Our issues are long-standing. I don't know where she and I will end up in all this, but that process is very separate from you. I'm just grateful that we share life paths, and I want to care for you for as long as I can, as I can."

His ability to live fully in the moment, without expectation, was helpful for me, as I was struggling to stay clear of defining my own expectations. I knew by now that I would be moving the girls and myself into an apartment within the next few months. I just had to work out how to do that. I had not shared this with him. He was still trying to sort out his own issues.

"I feel the same way," I said.

We continued to meet as often as our schedules allowed, although it was not every week. There was no structure to our conversations. We just talked about what happened to be on our minds that particular hour.

What developed on a deeper level was a growing trust, acceptance, and a willingness to be vulnerable. I felt that I had never experienced such closeness, connection, and sharing with anyone. This man was awakening me with the fullness of his presence, his passion for life, and his direct honesty. He touched something in my soul. He told me one day that he really enjoyed being able to "bump up against someone." That was a new expression for me. I understood it as feeling safe enough within a relationship to be fully oneself without fear of being judged—to be able to voice an opinion and have it heard and respected. I felt nourished within a growing relationship that led me into an absolute awareness of the core energy of another human being.

One day, we met in town to share a car as we had decided to drive a bit farther to a park just north of the city. We enjoyed our lunch and conversation, as always. It was a crisp fall day. We held hands as we walked slowly back to the car and got in to return to the city. Suddenly, Earle turned in his seat, his left hand on the steering wheel, looked directly at me, and said, "Will you help me die?"

The statement came out of nowhere. I was dumbfounded, held frozen. I was shaken. The question implied love, commitment, a lifetime. We had never talked of permanence, just our growing affection. This question came from somewhere deep within him.

I heard myself answer: "Yes."

CHAPTER 3

New Love and New Realities

It feels good to walk outside into the yard, away from the house, away from Earle, who is settled in front of the TV. The moon rises behind the palms and lights my way. The breeze is gentling for the night, and I feel bathed by the quiet. I have time and space to breathe. The path across the grass to my healing room is well worn now. It is my personal space, set apart from the house. I made this room my own, painting the inside in soft blue and filling it with furniture and objects that connect me with family and experiences that ground me. The humid subtropical air of deep-south Texas is sweet with flowering plants and holds the songs of night insects. I am drawn to my journal, where it waits for me and my questions. Who is this man I married just short of twenty years ago? This man who was my rock? Who am I now? Who are we now?

It is the first spring of 2000, a new decade. We are together now in the Rio Grande Valley, two years together after two years apart.

Those were long years from 1996 to 1998. Earle continued his work in Lexington at the University of Kentucky, and I was in Texas, building a new occupational therapy program. Earle continually searched for a position here, but nothing worked out.

Despite the challenges, we fell into a rhythm of sorts: Earle took road trips to Texas during his teaching breaks, and I flew to Lexington as often as my schedule allowed. We talked every evening, comparing our days. I was new at academic administration, and he was my mentor, guiding me through the intricacies of university politics and culture. I was so busy I barely had time to think. But time was heavy for him. Being alone became so hard that one day he told me he had adopted a dog that he named Slugger.

"It was just too hard."

Once, as we talked, I heard the gurgle of liquid being poured.

"What's that?" I asked.

"Just needed to refill my wine."

As time went on, I noticed I heard that sound more frequently.

There was a time when I thought seriously of leaving my position and returning to Kentucky. I knew I could find work and felt how hard it was for him. But then I had a dream. It was New Year's Eve 1997. I dreamed that Earle was retired, and I was still working. We had been living somewhere, then moved. I was not sure I wanted to live in the new place, but it was by an ocean with many small islands in the distance. In the dream, I discovered I was pregnant. The question became what to do about the pregnancy; to have an abortion or not. Then I woke up.

The dream stayed with me all day, and suddenly I understood: The pregnancy was my job, my new life growing here in the Rio Grande Valley—all the joy I had found here. To abort this pregnancy would terribly wound myself, and Earle. I was meant to carry my job to term and give birth to a healthy new life. Mine, and therefore his. Together we created this pregnancy. He was part of its creation as much as I was. To deny it would be to deny new life for both of us.

Our eagerness to be together was a powerful force, and he found the way—early retirement in 1998. I felt relieved. I would have support. I would no longer have to deal with everything alone.

Earle was to move to Texas in early June, and two weeks before, in our usual evening phone call, he paused.

"I just got some hard news."

Something stopped me cold.

"I have prostate cancer."

"What does that mean? For you? For us? Can you still come?" I was suddenly trying to make order out of flying thoughts. Trying to grab hold of the fear and disappointment and tie them down.

"The doctor said I can be treated in Texas, so we'll just have to find our way into that system and get it set up," he said.

⁂

Earle's move to Texas brought our belongings and dogs under the same roof, but it also brought a husband who was having X-rays aimed at his most private parts—lying spread out on a table, waiting for the machine to send the beams. Thirty-seven treatments were required. At first, it wasn't bad. But then came fatigue, urinary irritation, diarrhea, and leaking. An assault to manhood, an assault to body.

"Oh, damn. Not again," I heard him say one evening as I was preparing supper.

He pushed up out of the recliner, trying to hurry, bent over a bit, to the bathroom. Sounds of scurrying, clothing shifting. Then briefly, quiet.

"I didn't make it," I heard.

"I'm sorry," I said.

He cleaned up after himself, clothing, body, floor. I allowed him this—the ability to care for himself.

Radiation tired his body. We had looked forward to his retirement for so long, and all the magic that word meant: relaxation, freedom to explore, creating a new life.

"I wanted to be able to drive down to South Padre and just sit on the beach, or fish," he said. "Now I can't go anywhere where there isn't a toilet nearby. I'm so tired all the time. It's just so frustrating."

As that first summer back together went on, drinking, mood swings, and outbursts began to occur. When I reflected on it, this was reminiscent of other times, in Memphis and in Lexington, when stresses increased. I was often tense, never knowing if this was going to be a good day or a bad day. But I also noticed he looked forward to his treatments and was finding a social support system.

"The nurses and technicians all know me," he said. "I'm impressed at their skill. There are others I'm beginning to know too."

As he told me about the people he met, he described each one, reporting what they said in great detail and with much animation. Interaction with others energized him.

I tried to stay stable with my work, my mind. I felt bombarded. Office hours, meetings, preparing classes, eruptions of small fires that needed to be put out, phone calls—all the while trying to remain sensitive to my husband and his needs. There was no quiet place. I often pulled away from what felt like overstimulation by focusing on tasks that took no thought. Self-protection, I knew.

※

The confusion usually happened in the evening.

"What time is it?" he asked. "Aren't the Johnsons coming over?"

"They live in Lexington, honey. We're in Texas now."

"Oh, I thought we were supposed to give them something. What time did you say it was?"

Episodes like this were brief. I chalked it up to illness, fatigue, and depression, all of which could play havoc with memory. But after all those decades of experience as an occupational therapist, I knew to tuck this away as a concern.

※

Treatments ended in late summer of 1998, and we both relaxed with the expectation that the cancer was gone. Earle turned sixty in October, and my gift to him was a surprise birthday party. A nice crowd gathered in our small home, people he had come to know since his arrival four months earlier, and it was truly a surprise for him. Guests were faculty from the university where I worked, church members, and neighbors. He was the center of it all and was totally involved with the fun of it, laughing at gag gifts and friendly joking until the last person left.

"Thank you," he said. "I was really surprised, and I appreciate you doing that." He gave me a big hug. His body felt solid and strong.

That October we spent a week at a resort in Brownsville. Buildings were spread along *resacas*, inland waterways that stretched like fingers reaching in from the Gulf of Mexico.

The small porch, screened to keep the night insects out, felt cozy in the lovely early fall of the subtropics. It had been a restful day.

"Do you ever think back to our early days?" I asked.

"Yes, I do," he said with a softening of his face. "It seems so long ago now.

"Moving through the process of leaving my marriage, trying to understand it all. I remember I felt so guilty. I felt such a sense of failure, especially at letting my children down."

He reached across the arm of the canvas chair I was sitting in and folded my hand in his.

"But we were together all the way, weren't we?" he said. "I'm so grateful for you and for every day we have."

Together all the way? There was a surprising dissonance there for me in that moment. Yes, we had been together all the way, but I sensed that we were beginning to take different paths.

"I've always thought that our wedding was just as it should be," I offered up. "Mark was so proud to be your best man, and the girls were sweet, all dressed up. I liked Pastor Steven's comments, and Tye's organ music was full of his energy. We didn't need any more than that, did we?"

I settled back into my chair a bit more and drifted back into that time, seventeen years ago in Memphis.

～

Then, it was all about our newness and deepening love. One evening after dinner, during that time, we lingered over a glass of wine. Earle reached across the dining table and took my hand in his.

"All I know is to be as honest as I can be," he said. "I'm so grateful to have you in my life. You've shown me things about myself that I didn't know. You have become a part of my life that is beautiful. I treasure you."

His words echoed what was in my heart.

We knew by the middle of 1981 that we wanted to be married. Life got busy very quickly after that: Sorting out finances, getting to know each other's children, finding a place to live. We settled on a big, older home in downtown Memphis, not far from Earle's work and not far from the Mississippi River. It felt like the marriage ceremony on December 21, 1981, marked the end of a long time of waiting. We had established the feeling of partnership long before. On that day, Mark was fifteen, Mary was eleven, Michelle was nine, and Katie was eight.

Shortly before the wedding, Earle told me about something that had recently happened at work. He looked troubled. "The chancellor is leaving in the spring to take the same position at the University of Maryland. He asked if I would like to come with him. Said he'd create a position for me."

My heart landed in my stomach. "What did you tell him?"

"I said no. These children's lives have already been disrupted, and I just can't add to that."

I breathed a sigh of relief but also realized what a hard decision that must have been. The chancellor had been his mentor and supporter for years and years. To give up that relationship must have been very hard.

"We'll just have to see who the replacement will be," he said.

That concern shifted to the background as we looked forward to our new life.

⁂

Sitting on the patio in Brownsville, I startled out of my reverie into present time. Earle was slapping at an errant mosquito that had somehow found its way through the screen.

"Time to go inside?" I said.

"Maybe so. That one drew blood. And it's time for another beer."

Our room was designed like a small cabin. It was warm inside and welcoming, as the evening was getting cooler. Small table lamps created a soft yellow glow in the room. I snuggled into a big armchair with nubby brown covering and Earle found the recliner, settling back with a cold beer.

Still involved in my mental wanderings, I said, "The dinner at Paulette's after the wedding was really nice. The kids enjoyed that."

"It was, it was. They had such good food." Earle was still connected to his appetites.

"Do you remember all those early times with our kids?"

I looked over, saw Earle nodding off, let go of the conversation, and took my own self back into our first few months of marriage. It had been a cold winter in Memphis that year of 1981, with Christmas just passed.

"We've got to talk," I had said to Earle one evening after a stormy, child-leveled accusation that one of the "other" children had said something not nice.

"Triangulation," my new husband had said after thinking for a minute. "They'll try to put us in the middle, so we need to just tell them they can work it out and send them on their way."

That makes sense, I thought, grateful that he had been running conflict management workshops for a while, but also remembering my own professional training in interpersonal relationships.

"But," he said over his shoulder as he began to walk away, "if they draw blood, we can intervene." I saw the smile in his eyes and knew it would be OK.

So, our united message to all four children when they got into arguments was "You can work it out." And they did.

We had our own issues to sort through as we moved into problems and pressures of our own. Arguments popped up like firecrackers, sometimes unexpected and confusing. For me, the problems occurred mostly when Earle had been out with buddies and had a fair amount to drink. I would get anxious about whether he would get safely home, never knowing when that would be. When he came in the door, my anxiety spilled over.

"Where were you?" I said. "I've been waiting. I was worried."

"I was just out. You know my friends." He was loud, his mood surly, irritated, and we began to trigger each other. I had not seen this version of Earle when we were dating.

At another time when we were rested, I talked about this.

"Look," I said. "My father believed that children should never see parents fight. So, I never saw them fight. I don't know what to do when we get into these skirmishes, and it makes me feel awful. I want to work at trying to understand what's happening between us."

"I think we make assumptions about what the other person means without checking it out," he said. "We're just reacting to what we think is meant. I'd like to make a commitment to try and not make assumptions about what is going on, but to check it out instead."

I agreed to that commitment. It was hard to keep in mind, but we both worked at it and found that more often than not it helped.

As we continued to learn how to live together, this thought came to me one day: "You know, I think that when we argue we should ask ourselves, 'Does this reaction belong to me or to the previous relationship?'"

Earle considered that and said, "I think you've got something there. I'll make that part of my thinking as best I can."

"I will too."

And another agreement was made.

In Brownsville, I still roam through my memories. Memories of who we used to be, that is. But I also see who we are now. Earle is sixty-two, tired, with an ever-widening girth. Stuck. I am fifty-nine, feeling pride in what I have accomplished professionally, feeling creative and of value.

On the way home from our week at the resort, I hear, from out of the blue: "If I'm ever alone with that chancellor I would gut him."

The statement is hard, sudden, passionate. *Did our reminiscing trigger that outburst? Can he ever let go of the anger, the hurt*, I ask myself. It comes from such long-held memory.

The new chancellor for the university had arrived in summer 1982. I knew within the first year that Earle would have to leave and told him so. But he wasn't able to hear.

"He's sending out pink slips, closing down departments, moving people. I feel so bad for what's happening, but I think I might be OK." His body seemed always tense, and he was often irritable. Finally, well into the next year, Earle came home from work one day and said, "I'm going to look for another job." He threw his jacket on a chair.

"I support you in that, but what happened?" I asked.

"The chancellor asked me to develop a specific project to be reported to the board at their next meeting. I worked hard on it. I feel loyalty to this university and will work as hard as I can for it. The board meeting was this afternoon. I gave my report and in front of everyone, he looked at me and said that was not the information he asked me to develop and that I needed to do it again. I was dumbfounded, felt cut off at the knees. I just sat down."

I was aghast. What an incredibly horrible thing to do a man who wanted nothing more than to do his best.

"I can't believe he did that. That is absolutely cruel." I could barely contain my anger. "There are other places out there that would welcome you."

It was time to take serious action. In the meantime, he found relief from the stress of working with this new administrator by committing to never-ending new projects.

"I want to become a good biker," he said one day. "I've been researching the best road bikes, and I'll need to get biking shoes and some other things too."

All of this gear manifested within the next week. I looked out toward the driveway one afternoon, and there was my husband standing proudly next to a new bike, examining it with full absorption. I could almost see him thinking about kicking the tires. He wore black shoes, black biking shorts, and a close-fitting shirt, yellow across the midsection and black at the shoulders. Topping it off was a yellow helmet sitting squarely on his head. He was ready to go. I suddenly had an image of a very large bumblebee and lifted my hand to smother my smile.

Another day he said, "I'd like to get involved in training a German shepherd for Schutzhund," which I was to learn later was police dog work but also a competitive sport.

He researched the sport, filling me in on what he had learned. He found a Schutzhund training group in Memphis and with enthusiasm introduced me to a German shepherd puppy. I was hooked. We named her Sophia.

Then it was, "I've just agreed to coach a girls soccer team. Mary and Michelle are old enough to play. It's a great group of people."

And then, "I want us all to be involved with the Memphis Canoe Club. It would be great for the kids."

Earle did have a canoe. It sat out in the yard, propped against the side of the house.

"That's a really good canoe. Very sturdy," he said enthusiastically. "It's an Old Town. I couldn't afford one, so I became a dealer for the company here in Memphis and they gave me a great deal."

Expenditures racked up.

"Our finances are already stretched," I said one day. "Do we really need all of these things?"

"It's important to have safe and proper equipment and clothing. You always need the right tools for the job."

That was his theme.

One evening, as I sat in the dining room relaxing over a glass of wine, dinner dishes cleared away, I suggested, "Why don't I take over paying the bills and get that off your hands?"

"OK, but let me see how you're going to do it."

He came over to look. I showed him the method I used effectively and successfully for years. He blew up.

"That's not how you do it!" He stood over me, face flushed.

"But that's how I do it, and I've never had a problem."

"If you are going to do it, it has to be done this way," he said and proceeded to explain the way he wanted it done. Still angry but not quite as loud.

I agreed. *His way or the highway.*

∽

Insurance mechanisms in health care were changing. The large hospital system I worked for in Memphis instituted a quota system for the number of patients I was required to see in a day. It was beyond what was reasonable for effective treatment of people in distress and conflicted with my values. I thought about looking for another job.

Despite the continuing job stresses in Memphis during those early years, comfortable ways of blending our families began to form. Earle's son, Mark, and daughter, Michelle, and my daughters, Mary and Katie, were in familiar schools. Schedules generally worked out so that all four were with us every other weekend. One evening in late fall 1983, Earle walked into the kitchen and said, "Mark just called. He wants me to come get him."

"What do you mean? It's a weeknight. He has school tomorrow."

"There was urgency in the call," Earle said as he collected his car keys and put on a jacket. "He said 'come and get me now.' I've got to go."

I was taken by surprise. It was just short of Mark's seventeenth birthday. *Is he going to come permanently or is this an impulsive, short-term visit?*

Later that evening, they came in the door with a suitcase and bags of shoes and clothing. *Looks like this is long-term*, I thought and put fresh sheets on his bed.

"Life is not predictable, is it?" I said as I gratefully fell into bed that night.

"No. We'll just have to sort it out."

Earle's enthusiasm for life and all it had to offer made it hard not to become part of his excitement. I joined him in the training of three German shepherds in the Schutzhund program. It was interesting and I met a lot of good and dedicated people. The whole family got involved in the Memphis Canoe Club. We met great people, all interested in safe, outdoor family fun. The club ran trips to lovely rivers in northern Arkansas and the Missouri boot heel, and all the children took basic canoe courses. We camped, had picnic lunches, and grilled burgers and hot dogs in the evenings after getting off the river. A number of the people involved were also colleagues of Earle's, and my social world expanded.

I even got talked into a whitewater class II river course.

"I cannot believe myself, standing here in the middle of February next to a raging river, dressed in a black rubber wet suit, about to climb into a canoe with my stepson. I'm trying to think of this as a bonding experience," I said. I was shivering with the chill, not excitement.

Earle laughed. "You'll do just fine."

Mark and I only got dumped out of the canoe once. It was something I would never have done on my own, and I was surprised how much fun it was.

Job searches continued. It was hard to stay centered, but life with the children stabilized. We settled into routines and patterns and began to cement relationships.

We were six people brought together in a relatively short period of time. The adults wanted to be together. The four children were told their lives were now different. Each set of two was raised by one parent very different than the one they now found themselves with. There were tensions, arguments, and misunderstood communications.

"It's time for a family meeting," Earle said one evening when an argument broke out about scheduling laundry times. He directed everyone to sit down in the living room, and one-by-one, each person said what he or she thought about the issue. Everyone had a voice. Then Earle asked for ideas, and again, everyone had a voice. A solution was worked out, pretty much managed by the children. After this, family meetings became a part of our lives together.

We both tried hard to find comfortable and loving ways of being with each other's children. Earle and I supported all four of them in their school and athletic interests. We stayed involved. But the stresses were real. I noticed that when Earle was tired, or had had a fair amount of wine with dinner, he sometimes lashed out at Mary or Katie. This happened rarely, but I could see the hurt in their faces before they withdrew to their rooms. One evening, I asked him why.

"Mary was playing games," he said. "She was manipulating."

"Earle, she's twelve. I didn't see any of that." It was clear to me he didn't hear. He had had a lot of wine.

That evening, I saw the fallacy of my fantasy. I thought that because Earle and I loved each other, all four children would also love us and each other. How wrong I was.

I moved into support mode. The people I loved were struggling.

"I think I'm caught in the Equal Opportunity vise," Earle said one evening. "I've been a semifinalist for three positions and in each case the person hired was a woman or African-American. I don't know how I will ever get out of this. I just have to try and hang in there."

I noticed more gray in his beard, his widening midline, his tense body; a man adrift and in distress.

"It will work out, I'm sure," I said. But I was concerned. His energy and mood were low. He was quick to get irritable and angry, and evenings out with buddies became a bit more frequent. Abundant beer was always a part of these social times.

Michelle, on a weekend visit in January of 1985, announced that she was not going back to her mother's house. It was sticky to work out, but suddenly we became a full-time family of six.

Pressures were building as our lives became more complex. It was almost inevitable something would burst. It turned out it would be me.

The day it happened, I had been busy with new patients and talks about meeting treatment quotas. I was tired to begin with and came home exhausted. I walked in the door to a house full of teens playing boom boxes at the highest decibels, dogs wanting attention, the children's debris everywhere, and everyone hungry.

"Stop! Stop it all now." I heard myself, not recognizing the person screaming. I was in psychic pain. All of me hurt. I had always been acutely sensitive to sound, and the cacophony was overwhelming.

"Turn off the music," I said, still loud. "You may play your music from now on in your rooms only, doors closed."

Suddenly, silence.

Earle walked in, took one look at me, and said, not unkindly but firmly, "Get in the car. I'll be right out."

"I can't. I've got to get dinner going."

"Get in the car. I'll be right out."

I was so exhausted, so worn out, that I couldn't argue anymore. I went to the car.

Earle appeared in a few minutes. "Here, hold these."

He handed me a cold jug of white wine, which seemed to occupy a permanent place in our refrigerator, and two wine glasses.

"Where are we going?"

"You'll see."

He drove down to the Mississippi, to a small park on a bluff overlooking the river. He parked, took the jug of wine and glasses, and led me across the grass to a green wooden bench that had an open view of the bridge and the river traffic. It was quiet. No one else there, just birds and the sun beginning to set. An occasional breeze stirred in the trees overhead. He poured the wine and I noticed the sound, musical. He put a glass in my hand but didn't say a word.

We sat for a while, sipping our wine, and slowly, slowly, I felt my muscles begin to loosen. My breath came more evenly and deeply. I gave myself up to the rhythm of the river, carrying vessels of all sizes to faraway places.

Finally, I was able to say, "Some days I just don't know how I can make it. I get so, so tired. I feel like there is no resting place." I wept quiet tears then.

"You know, our kids aren't little anymore," Earle said. "They get home from school before we get home from work. Why don't they cook their own dinner?"

I stopped to think. *Could they do that? How would it work? Would they get enough to eat?* "Maybe we could put them in charge of working out all the details and see what they come up with. Do you think that might work?"

"I do. Let's talk with them about it when we get back," he said.

It worked. The four young people organized it all, made charts and menus, and assigned cooking days for each one.

As the months passed, the job hunting went on. The not-knowing was very stressful. More gray hairs appeared on our heads. We both gained weight. New lines appeared in our faces. We struggled with these changes, acutely aware of them. We were not new anymore, but we were surviving. I realized that I expected us to stay young forever and felt the loss of that dream. The children were stable. We had jobs. But the constant financial strain ate away at us, especially me.

I'm good at seeing to the needs of everyone in the family, I thought. I knew I was not good at caring for myself. But Earle, especially when he was rested and having better days at work, was able to somehow see me.

"We gift each other," I said one night as we lay together in the afterglow of loving. "I feel so cared for. You're my closest friend."

"I got a letter today from the University of Kentucky!" Earle was almost dancing.

I was so happy for him. It was fall 1986, and he was invited to accept a position with that university beginning in January 1987. And so, we would move to Lexington. Our prayers were answered.

※ ※ ※

Now, this evening in a new millennium, two years together in Texas, those Memphis years a lifetime ago, I hear the scratch of palm fronds rubbing together in the night breeze. I notice the scent of the herbs that fill my basket on the floor, set down my pen, close my journal, and stretch. I look around my small room and see the painting I completed after our vacation in Brownsville. The view is from the edge of the resaca, ducks swimming lazily by in the water against a backdrop of the setting sun. It is a bearer of memories.

I step into the cool night, feeling the fresh air on my skin, and walk through the yard, back toward the house and my husband, who is probably dozing in front of the TV. Did I miss the signs? The sudden outbursts, the overspending, the overcommitment. Or am I seeing a man under great stress? I delay judgment, knowing that I, too, had times when I was terribly stressed, reacting with as much passion as he did. What I had seen come through in the words I set down in my journal this night was a loving, caring, passionate man who lived with integrity, honoring his family and his work. That is the man I married.

CHAPTER 4

Rock Formation

Our prayers were answered. Or so we thought.

Lexington was beautiful. Acres and acres of gentle green pasture. Sleek horses quietly grazing. Immense white barns, white fencing. Clean. A sense of order. At one thoroughbred horse farm, chandeliers hung in the cupolas of the barn. A warm glow from them lit the night. Someone told me a sheik owns the farm. Quite a change from Memphis, its surrounding cotton farms, the river, the jazz scene, the diversity, and the not-so-well-hidden poverty.

Earle and I began to work out plans for our new life.

"I think I should find a furnished apartment until the house sells and we get the girls moved here," he said.

Mark had already moved out, on his own, back in Memphis. He had an apartment and a steady job. The only one of us settled.

"That makes sense," I said. "I think, too, that we should bring the girls here for a visit to look at schools. Maybe if they find one they like, we can look for a house in that district."

Our announcement about the impending move had been met with a unified cry of protest. Resistance was too light a word. Their lives were disrupted, after all. Mary was sixteen, Michelle was fifteen, and Katie was thirteen.

I stayed in Memphis with our daughters for six months until the house sold. Earle started his job in Lexington and drove to Memphis for weekends as often as he could. It was hard to be apart. All of us were in a change curve, with our anchors shifting. I was so grateful for his visits. When he arrived, he was totally present for me—caring, thoughtful, engaged, loving. His touch was nourishing and healing. When he shared his concerns, I was reminded of the magic of us. That flow of energy, that sharing that was our beginning.

"Money is tight for the university," he said one day. "The state has mandated budget cuts, and one of my first responsibilities is to lay off forty-eight people. It's so hard to do. These are people with families. I'm hoping I can find other places for them in the system."

I heard the caring concern in his tone. I saw it in his troubled expression. He had been very involved with his large staff in Tennessee and saw them as family. That's just who he was.

"I'm so sorry that has to be," I said, taking his hand. "I hope you can work something out for them."

"I'm not sure where I fit, either," he continued. "I don't see the chancellor very often and have been connected with his assistant, instead, as the person I should deal with. He and the chancellor have worked together for a long time. It's awkward."

"I can see that's hard for you," I offered, knowing his need for inclusion.

∼

We wintered in different states for that first part of 1987. In my time alone in Memphis, I found myself questioning: *What do I want to do with who I am?* This was a change point, I knew. An opportunity to create something new.

But those aspirations got ground down by the day-to-day management of keeping the house clean in case someone came by to look at it, preparing meals, and seeing to the needs of the children. Added in were my work and balancing a somewhat complicated budget, now split between two states. As was my fashion, I just kept going until one day I hit overload.

I rushed into a department store needing some new underwear and had just a window of time to find what I needed. The salesperson was distracted by something when it was my turn to pay.

"I'm in a hurry," I said, plunking the purchases and my purse down on the counter like a punctuation mark.

"Be right with you," she said.

"I've got kids at home, waiting for dinner," I said, my tone demanding now. No smile.

"I said, I'll be right with you." Her tone changed and grated on me. She rang up my few purchases, but it seemed she moved very slowly.

"Are you new?" I said. I could hear the edge in my voice.

"No, ma'am," she replied, syllables now drawing out. "I've been working here for five years." She handed me the bag.

"You might need a refresher course," I said over my shoulder as I spun away, my body tight and hard.

When I got to the car I climbed in and sat there, stunned. *That was not me! I was ugly to that woman. I never talk to people that way. I cannot believe how I behaved.* I felt so bad. Ashamed. Shocked. Why? Then a thought.

Stress. Sudden empathy for my husband. All those years of trying to find a new position. New understanding.

⁂

By late spring, the house in Memphis sold—at a loss. It was a trying time, but I found support through friends at work and the networking that occurs in a professional clinical community. I did have people to talk to who understood, and I was grateful for them. The girls finished the school year, and we worked out their summer schedules with their other parent. I organized and managed the move, ended my work in Memphis, and found a job in Lexington. We moved into a rented house, giving ourselves a year to find something more permanent.

Rock Formation

※

Lexington promised to be a good place for us. The scenery was beautiful, set in a community of long-established patterns built around horses, basketball, and the university. Was this the place? The place where each of us would be happy and fulfilled?

Within that peaceful place, though, the bedrock of my life began to shift. Seismic forces pushed against all of us—the shifting needs and growing pains of adolescents who did not want to move, finding our place—all those things that cannot be planned. We all felt overwhelmed.

One evening after dinner, I was finally relaxing in my favorite stuffed chair. Before Earle could pick up the TV remote, I wandered into what had been on my mind.

"I've become aware of how cut off from the world I've been," I began. "Wrapped up in job and family. I feel like I want to expand out beyond all of this. But I don't know what I want to do with my future. I don't know what I want to do with who I am."

"Is there any way I can help?" He put down the remote. "You know I'll support you in any way I can."

"I know you will. I just need to do some more thinking about all of this. I don't even know what direction I want."

I felt the tugs inside of me. I felt myself trying to realign who I knew myself to be in the face of all the other forces appearing on the horizon.

Financial stressors again became predominant. We'd lost money on the sale of the house in Memphis, and while both of us, theoretically, were hired at a nice increase in salary, we did not figure in the Kentucky state income tax, which left us on par with the situation we'd left. We faced moving costs and needs of growing children in addition to everything else.

On a walk one lovely, warm spring evening Earle suddenly announced, "I feel like it would be better for all of you if I did myself in. You would have my life insurance, and that would help with bills. I just don't see where I'm going with this job, and I can't make enough money to support us all."

I was shocked. I had seen him depressed during the Memphis years, but never anything like this. I didn't know what to say. I was angry with him for even suggesting such a thing and was scared by the depth of his depression.

"You need to get some help. See a counselor," I said firmly. "You know I'm with you in whatever comes our way, but what you're suggesting is not an answer. You need help."

We finished our walk in silence. He did not see a counselor, but gradually his mood lifted. Still, I was left shaken and with a new fear in my heart.

That first spring and summer in Lexington, Earle and I had to renew and re-work our relationship with each other and with our children. The half-year separation had seen changes in everyone's lives.

Earle found an outlet.

"I've joined the tennis club," he announced with excitement one evening when he came home from work. "They've got leagues set up, and maybe you can take lessons there and play too."

I thought, *Where will I ever find the energy for another new learning?*

Mary and Michelle, though, led us into a new form of being together. They came home from school one day early in the new school year, almost bouncing.

"We made the team," said Michelle, grinning from ear to ear.

"What team?" I said.

"The junior varsity soccer team!"

We supported them all the way, becoming part of the parents' booster club, helping to line fields, and cheering them at every game. Soccer provided a distraction from other pressures and allowed us to meet a lot of friendly people. That helped us through the fall.

December 21, 1987: Our sixth anniversary. Earle was forty-nine and I was forty-six. Time for review. Earle was more peaceful in his job. I was becoming tired of clinical practice. Children were beginning to pull away into their own transitions. We decided to go out on a date for our anniversary and gave ourselves a dinner at a nice restaurant made cozy with rich mahogany décor and red carpeting that muffled sound. We took a long while over dinner, just talking about whatever came up. It felt good to have a time that was not rushed.

"You know, something happened while I was still in Memphis and you were here, that was helpful to me," I said. I described my experience in the department store and how awful I had been. "I got a glimpse, I think, of how grinding and draining it was for you to go through those years of job search. It helped me understand you."

"Those years were tough." He laid his fork down on his plate. "I know I wasn't easy to live with sometimes. I can't tell you how important your support was to me. It helped me get by."

I took his hand, and we sat in companionable silence.

That Christmas was hard. We struggled to find our way financially to buy gifts we knew the girls and Mark wanted. It was important for me to give to those I loved at Christmas.

"How are we going to do this?" I said. "We've spent so much on tennis club dues and equipment and soccer gear for the girls, and track clothes and shoes for Katie. We've never caught up from the move."

"Well, all of those things are needed," Earle said. "It's about safety and the right equipment for the event."

But when I sat down to pay bills, I was always playing with ways to not get behind. It was a boulder on my back.

Seasons sped by, and it seemed like in no time we were at the end of the summer of 1988. I could not pretend anymore that all was well in Lexington. Earle and I were in and out of depression and were always tired. I found a new position as assistant professor at Eastern Kentucky University, a half-hour-drive away. I loved the change and was excited about the new learning, but I was expending a great deal of energy in meeting the challenge. Our financial situation was always there, in the shadows.

It felt like all five of us were hanging on by our fingernails, trying to find our way.

Mary came home from school one day, disgusted. "They don't even play any good rap music on the radio here."

Katie chimed in. "Yeah, and when I try and talk to the black kids in school they just turn away," she said. "It's not like it was back home."

I was at a loss, feeling my own absence of anchors. All I could say was, "It will get better," making myself believe that platitude. But I could see we were all equally lost in our own upheavals. It seemed like our lives were becoming more complex with all of us crisscrossing each other without much order.

I felt like my whole world was coming apart, scattered, out of control. I was spinning so fast that I was about to be ejected from our orbit. I tried to hold it all together and couldn't. I carried such a sense of failure. I tried so hard, but all of my dreams, hopes, and prayers didn't work. I wanted everyone to be happy, and no one was, and I couldn't fix it.

That Saturday had been a normal sort of day. I was doing laundry, a familiar and routine chore that always made me feel anchored and organized. Katie had invited two school friends over, and I was pleased, reading it as a sign of growing connection in our new community. The girls were talking and laughing in Katie's room, then came out looking for something to eat. The three of them walked down the hall toward the kitchen, chatting away, laughing, not paying any attention to Lady, my German shepherd, who was also in the rather narrow hallway. Lady was one of our shepherds who had been trained in Schutzhund. Part of the training involved attack and takedown of a human target. I saw a subtle shift in the dog's muscles, a tightening. Her eyes locked in on the motions of hands flying. She padded silently up to one of the girls and deliberately snapped at her hand. The girls did not notice. I called to Lady sharply. Her concentration shifted and she came to me, obediently. I took her outside.

"We're going to have to get rid of Lady," I said to Earle when he got home from playing tennis later that afternoon.

He looked surprised. "Why?"

"I saw her snap at one of Katie's friends. The liability of having a big dog that snaps at children is too much." I felt like my heart was breaking.

"Are you sure?" He offered nothing else. Too numb with his own burdens.

"Can you think of anything else we can do?" I asked again the next day.

"No, I really can't," he replied.

I placed Lady on Craigslist and waited a week. No takers. I called the police K-9 unit and offered her to them. They took her away to evaluate and brought her back a few days later saying she was already too old for the work. I could not bear the thought of a child being maimed and saw no other possibility but to have her euthanized. It was so hard. I loved that dog and agonized for over two weeks before coming to a final decision. I felt shut off from everyone, having gotten no support or meaningful response from Earle. I told the girls only after I had made the decision, explaining why. I wanted to protect them from the loss and took her to the vet alone. My friend. A final, heart-breaking loss in a year of lost hopes.

I can see now that my not asking anyone else for help, or just dropping the issue with Earle, was part of a deeper problem that was beginning to build. But I didn't know that then. The only thing I knew was that I felt without connection to anyone. It was a terrible feeling, but I did not have the mental flexibility to look beyond my own walls of stress and rigidity.

Lady was the tip of the iceberg of all the things we weren't talking about, couldn't talk about.

∽

The cool of autumn 1988 brought freshness to our lives. We found a small house within our budget. It was on a quiet street with a small stream running along beside it. It would be a new start for all of us.

Earle seemed to be finding more peace in his work

"The chancellor and I have moved into a pretty good working relationship," he said after dinner one evening. "It feels smoother and we've been able to move forward on some issues."

"I'm so glad for you," I said, meaning it. "It's been a long time coming."

As Earle felt more comfortable in his work, he was again able to give more support to me, listening to my thoughts, caring and accepting. I was relieved to have my partner back, to feel that I was not alone in dealing with what came our way. I was able to relax.

Mother's Day 1989. The three girls and I were gathered under a beautiful flowering crabapple that graced the front lawn of our new home. I was wearing a plum-colored blouse, my current favorite color, and a long skirt with a cream background and plum-colored flowers scattered over it. Earle had a new camera and was busy taking photos. It felt good to dress up and be arm-in-arm with our daughters. Earle had presented me with a vase full of red roses that morning, and I felt happy and appreciated. It had been ten years since Earle and I began having lunches together, but it seemed like yesterday.

Even as our lives smoothed out, patterns emerged as inexorable as the forces that shape the landscape of the earth. I rolled through periodic waves of depression spawned by exhaustion. The work of hewing out my place in this community and in my position at the university was exhausting. It was all new—nothing familiar. But such times were relieved with moments of fun, finding something to laugh at with the girls, sometimes watching a movie together, getting a good night's sleep. A mourning dove laid two eggs in a planter hanging on the deck before new spring growth emerged. I was fascinated. The dove did not move from her incubating, and I could get within two feet of her before I saw her tense. The baby birds finally emerged, and Earle's newest gadget—a video recorder—fit the bill. I taped hours of baby bird growth. The girls laughed at me, delighting in pointing out my compulsive ways.

Lulled by what seemed to be increasing peace in this new job, I shouldn't have been surprised by lapses into Earle's old patterns of depression. They were similar to the times in Memphis when he became depressed with the frustration of trying to find a new job while struggling to stay loyal to his current one. He would become irritable, losing himself in a glass of wine and TV rather than talking about what was on his mind. I had hoped that his new job, in a new community, would bring some improvement in his moods. However, depressions still occurred as he tried to find a way through a system different from the one in which he had spent seventeen years. All relationships were new; political alliances were new. He seemed unsettled.

I longed for our early times in Memphis.

~·~

"Surprise," everyone shouted. It was Earle's forty-fifth birthday, and I had arranged a party. Our home back then was filled with dear friends, people from the canoe club, the soccer community, and the university. It was October, and the air outside was crisp; but inside, the dark hardwood floors, glowing gas fireplace, oriental throw rugs, comfortable furniture, and window seats wrapped us in warmth. The table was loaded with good food and a cake decorated with a man kicking a soccer ball.

There was no mistaking the affection everyone had for Earle and for each other. It felt like family. These people had worked and played together for years and had built a community based on respect.

"I sure hope we can work out a fishing trip to Canada one day," Jim said to Earle.

"That would be so much fun," Earle said. "For me, it's a lifelong dream to spend a week with you and Larry, Dan, and Don. Let's keep that in mind."

Comfortable conversation among longtime friends.

With the move to Lexington, we had lost those threads that had woven us together.

~·~

Much later, I thought back to that party. Our children, with perhaps the exception of Mark, who was a bit older, were unaware of this part of Earle's world—the respect and affection people had for him. They were children who saw a big, strong man with mood swings, who caused me continual concern with his spending.

~·~

In a rare moment of quiet that allowed time for some reflective discussion, Earle and I were able to do some honest sharing. The girls were off in their rooms, busy with homework, and we had the living room to ourselves. Lamps softened the deepening shadows of evening.

"The 'not good' rating I got from the chancellor in my performance review in January really troubles me," he said. "I just don't know what I'm doing wrong or what I have to do to measure up. In all my years in Memphis, until the new chancellor came, I always got the highest ratings. It's really discouraging and frustrating."

"I know it is, sweetheart. I wish there was something I could do to help."

I got up and walked around behind his chair and rubbed his shoulders, feeling the tightness in his muscles. I, too, was troubled by the news.

"You can keep that up though," he said with a contented groan. "It does help."

When my hands got tired, I sat down.

"Teaching is getting better for me," I said. "I'm beginning to get a feel for the flow of the semester and am starting to understand how to structure material on a level that's understandable for the students. I was told if I could do it, I could teach it. How wrong that is. What I know about occupational therapy treatment is intuitive, I've been doing it so long. Now I have to break it all down to the most basic steps, and that's hard work."

"Oh, I know," he said with feeling. I knew that he did and felt comforted.

"I just get so very, very tired," I said, near tears. "I know I push myself, but there's so much going on. I want to do a good job at work, and the house needs to be taken care of, and I worry about the girls. It's been so hard for them to make this transition. Away from all that is familiar to them. I know they're still angry."

"Sweetheart, you've got to take care of yourself. The girls will be fine. What can I do to support you?"

"I don't know," I said. "I just don't know."

He took my hands in his. The warmth and solid strength of his touch was an anchor for me.

※

Mary's graduation from high school in May 1989 was a ray of sunshine. It felt so good to come together for her in support of her success. She was accepted by a good college, only about two hours' drive from us, and with the generous financial support of her father, she was able to attend. We could not have paid her tuition or dorm costs.

Financial pressures never let up. Somehow there was always at least one bill that could not be paid on time. I got very creative with juggling amounts and due dates and, somehow, we got by. Earle kept spending and always had involved rationalizations as to why. But for me, the situation was unrelentingly stressful.

Soon after 1990 rolled in, Earle came home one evening and said, "The university is providing a new medically managed weight loss program that our insurance will cover. What do you think about investigating it?"

I was excited to hear about that. Our weight was up, and we were not exercising at all.

"Great," I said. "I don't feel healthy right now."

"Neither do I. Let's do it."

Over the course of that year, we lost a significant amount of weight, began running, and altered our eating style. A new beginning. We would come home from work and run five miles, and we were fit enough to talk while we ran.

One evening as we ran, I said, "I can't remember when I have felt physically this good."

"There's a 5K coming up soon. Let's try it," said Earle.

"That's a good idea," I said. "It would be fun to do together."

One weekday evening, dinner finished, the girls doing the dishes, Earle and I sat in the living room, just unwinding. I settled into the big blue armchair. The girls finally went off to tackle homework. Suddenly I found myself removed, watching this scene from far away.

Something is not right with my family. We seem to be separate entities spinning in our little universes with no communication or cohesion. We talk and exchange information but there is no kindness, no warmth, no touch. We are wooden. I am troubled about the emotional health of all of us. Something is missing. What is it? Love?

I did not share these thoughts with anyone. But I did become aware of my own pattern of allowing myself to be drawn into the middle of tensions that arose between Earle and the girls. I intervened when I thought they were becoming angry or irritated with one another—trying to smooth things over, making excuses, creating explanations for behavior. One day in March, I announced to everyone at dinner, including Earle, "I'm going to stop putting myself in the middle of issues that come up between you all. You will have to work things out for yourselves."

There were some wide eyes at that, and I knew they heard my resolve. What I said in that moment was exactly what Earle and I had agreed to tell the children when we first married. I saw that I had been participating in triangulation.

On a balmy late-summer evening, Earle walked into the kitchen as I was cooking and casually said, "I'm going to have to start moving things around in the garage to make room for the Shopsmith."

"What's a Shopsmith?" I said.

With excitement and a waving of arms he said, "It's a piece of machinery that does all kinds of things. It's got a lathe and a band saw, other kinds of saws. You can build furniture, shelving, all kinds of things. I've always wanted to do woodworking."

He had talked about enjoying working with wood but never mentioned this piece of equipment to me. I spun around, furious.

"How much is it?" I demanded.

"About $1,500. But I've worked out a payment plan with them. I can pay it off over time."

"You find a way to pay it off because there's no room in our budget for another payment. I cannot believe you did this." I heard myself shouting.

"I'm sure we can find a way to handle it. It will all work out," and he left the room. I stood there, stunned. All I could think was, *Our debt load is eating me alive.*

Late summer melted into early fall. The chrysanthemums burst into glorious color in the front yard. Leaves began their softening from rich greens to golden browns with an occasional dash of brilliant red. The debt issue returned to its dark hiding place in my mind. There were bumps and tensions with the girls, but time with Earle again felt restoring and nourishing.

Michelle had graduated from high school in May and was off to the college in Alabama where her parents had gone. Her mother had found ways, through friends, to find financial support, as we again had very scarce resources.

I scheduled a routine physical at the university, and an eager young resident asked when I had my last mammogram. I thought I had remembered one three years before and he said, "Well, let's get one done."

Not long after, I came home to a letter from the medical center. I nervously opened it. The letter said I would need additional views.

It's cancer.

At that moment, I had no wish to fight. *Death would be peace. The girls are healthy and close to independence. I left my former husband what was most important to him—the house. I took what was most important to me—my children. Earle will have my life insurance, which will bail him out.*

I asked myself: *Where am I in all this? What is my role? What do I enjoy? Where can I find the will to live? We need help. How do I confront this?*

I told Earle about the letter when he got home but did not share my thoughts.

"Well, we just have to follow up. It may be nothing." He wrapped his arm around my shoulders.

In mid-September 1990, I had a needle biopsy that showed two kinds of breast cancer. One was the most common, DCIS-ductal cell in situ. The other was Comedo, more aggressive and difficult to treat. For this reason, the doctors recommended a mastectomy. They also suggested reconstruction, and I was evaluated as being a good candidate for a TRAM flap—transverse rectus abdominus—because of my excellent physical condition. This is a procedure in which a portion of the rectus abdominus muscle is moved, with skin and blood supply intact, up under the skin into the space left by the mastectomy. My doctors had assured Earle and me that, pending pathology results, the prognosis looked good.

I was overwhelmed. *What do I do with this?* I had never experienced a major surgery and had no coping skills, no tools for a procedure that had such import. I had never been sick other than usual childhood illnesses. I searched for the why of it, aware of the string of stressful life events over the past fifteen years. I knew about the links between stress and its effect on the immune system. I was very aware of my decreasing reserves of energy.

I needed to give—to be the strong one all these years. Now, the children were healthy and stable, husband was stable, jobs were stable, but I was sick. After a long, sleepless night wrestling with these realities, I suddenly became clear that my task was to build my arsenal of healing. I must look at my life and gather around me all the positive resources I could find to help me heal.

As I waited for the surgery date, busyness was my salvation—a place to hide. I escaped to the familiar, the routine household tasks that belonged to me and gave some structure to the chaos. As I waited, I vacillated between scared and peaceful. I was scared of scaring Katie. I was scared that I might die.

Our good friend Janie came by to visit. She talked about something she had read that was actually written for parents of children who were born with a handicap. The parents grieved not for their child but for the loss of the dream of what might have been. That touched something deep inside, and I knew that this was part of my upheaval: the loss of the dream of myself as someone who was strong, resilient, capable, healthy, energetic.

⁂

My colleagues at Eastern Kentucky University threw a party the night before the surgery. They showered me with funny cards. The evening reminded me of the words of a pastor from my early years in Memphis, before I met Earle. Often at the end of each service, the pastor left us with a powerful image: "Imagine God's arms around you, supporting you, through all your days."

I held that image in my mind as I entered surgery. God's arms as well as those of family and friends, wrapped around me.

Rock Formation

~

On October 3, three months short of my fiftieth birthday, I underwent a mastectomy and breast reconstruction, which took eleven hours to complete.

During that time, Earle was my rock. It had been an emotional roller coaster, but he offered strength. He was a positive presence, always supportive and comforting. He was my predictable, steady place and never once strayed from his message that I would be fine. He repeated that every time I wavered. He heard my struggle and was there, present with me, always with reassurance. He was my strength when I could not find it.

~

One morning, about a week after I came home from the hospital, Earle rolled over and began gently touching me, stroking me—as man and woman, husband and wife. What a moving and wonderful experience. This simple touch restored my personhood, my dignity, and my humanity. My body had been assaulted, hurt, stared at, bandaged. All without caring touch. How wonderful for my husband to accept me back, with loving tenderness. He still found my carved-up body beautiful.

The strain of the unexpected diagnosis, the long hours of surgery, and being always the strong support for me affected him. In those days I did not know where his support was, and during these months I did not fail to notice. He began to gain weight again, leaving behind a healthy eating pattern of several years. He was struggling. He faced work stresses. For a week or two after the surgery I could not help at home with meals, nor could he handle those household tasks.

Once the surgery was in the past, and it was clear I would survive, it was Earle's turn to fall apart. Katie's too. My youngest daughter grew quieter, withdrawing from us. She was the only daughter still at home, and it fell to her to be the one to clean my hundreds of stitches twice a day, because I couldn't see all of them. She was just sixteen. There was no one there to be the rock for her. Cancer affects everyone.

The first week, the chancellor's wife organized a week of meals for us—a huge help. Entering the second week, I saw I could manage simple meals. My inherent eagerness for life pushed me forward into reconnecting with the needs of my family through normal daily tasks.

I still hurt everywhere. That is what was real. In the first few weeks of healing, my body was the focus. Because I was an occupational therapist, I knew how to manage movement and so was essentially independent after about ten days at home. I measured my improvement increment by increment. Yet all of my body mechanics had shifted because of the rearrangement of my abdominals, and for two weeks I couldn't stand up straight because stitches were pulled so tight. I thought I could walk a mile, and I tried, but the result after two blocks was exhaustion and back pain.

In those first few weeks and months, my endurance was very poor. I tired quickly, and even simple tasks were exhausting. I found that I was weak, vulnerable, dependent, and slowed. I had met the reality of an altered self-image, the unrealistic expectations I had of myself as resilient Wonder Woman. I had lost what I knew as my self.

"Trust the process," friends and doctors said.

I found I had a great deal of trouble trusting the process because I wanted to control it. I thought, *How much of my life energy have I given to trying to control people and events?* I also became aware that sitting back and not being always busy allowed me to give much more time to Earle and Katie.

After three weeks at home, I decided I was going to be normal. My plan was to nourish my body and regain my pre-op fitness. I went back to work at four weeks.

One evening at dinner, not long after returning to work, I burst into tears.

"What's wrong, sweetheart?" Earle said.

"I'm all patched together. Things are not right. And nobody sees, so they think I'm fine. I'm not getting better." I was still crying.

Earle replied with a gentle but firm voice, blue eyes holding mine. "You are getting better. What you don't yet have is a reserve. You used all of that in coping with the trauma of the surgery and you just have to rebuild."

His perspective was helpful. It eased me.

It was scary to allow myself to be dependent on others for some things—to be vulnerable, needing help. But I found I didn't need to run away from that. And finally, for the first time in my life, I understood what it was like to lean on someone else's strength. I needed Earle. I needed his strength, patience, and wisdom. I also began to understand that I didn't always need to be there to support everyone else. I could trust others to support me.

I was beginning to rebuild my physical self, walking for several miles every day, then beginning to run again. I knew that the emotional rebuilding would take much longer. The "whole" had been shattered into the sum of its parts.

CHAPTER 5

A Glimmer of New Perspectives

I fold into my favorite time of the year here in the Rio Grande Valley—early spring. Peace inhabits the space that has become my healing room, the rich scent of citrus blossoms entering through open windows. The year 2000 brings hope for a less-turbulent time. I live in gratitude and find joy in the culture of this community, ten miles from the Mexican border. I have grown used to traveling the short distance to the bridge into Mexico, enjoying the *chiles rellenos*, Mexican guitar, and warmth of the people. But now I am pulled back, remembering.

On a fine spring day in 1991, I came upon Earle poring through fishing equipment with single-minded focus. He had pulled tackle boxes and fishing poles from the garage and spread them out in the driveway.

"Looks like a fishing trip coming soon," I said.

"Yeah. I'm thinking I'll head over to Taylor Lake and see if anything's biting."

A Glimmer of New Perspectives

"Can I come with you sometime?" I asked, surprising myself.

"Sure, that would be great," he said. "We can go tomorrow, but we'll have to leave about three in the morning."

"What?"

"Well, it's a two-hour drive and we've got to get there by sun-up when the fish start biting."

He was totally serious. I weighed my response. I was not a morning person.

"I can do it if I can sleep in the back seat on the way there," I said.

He looked surprised but nodded his acceptance.

We set off at three the next morning in Earle's pickup, pulling his johnboat, which he had hooked to the hitch the night before. I headed for the back seat and quickly fell into a sound sleep. Two hours later, the slowing of the truck and the crunching gravel pulled me out of my dreams, and I saw we were next to water. Faint fingers of orange-gold light reached into the fading night sky.

"I need your help," Earle said. "I'm going to back the trailer down the boat ramp into the water, and I'll need you to hold onto that rope tied to the front of the boat as it slides off the trailer so it won't drift away."

OK, pretty straightforward. I grabbed hold of the scratchy rope. I felt water come up over my sneakers at the top of the ramp but was caught by how the morning light created lovely shades of green and violet. I heard the truck start up. It all happened so fast. The strong tug of the boat as it slid off the trailer surprised me, and suddenly I was sitting waist deep in water on the boat ramp, which was slick with algae. I burst out laughing.

"Well, you held onto the rope," Earle said, grinning. He took the rope from me, grabbed my hand, and pulled me up. "Good you've got a change of clothes. Now we go get the bait."

I changed into a dry shirt and shorts behind the open truck door, and then off we went to the bait shop for fishing licenses and bait. The shop was a small, one-story wooden building with weatherworn boards and was filled with an overwhelming array of all things to do with fishing. I recognized very little except for buckets of worms and cages of crickets. Earle paid for the fishing licenses and a cage of crickets.

"They're alive," I said. I caught the almost-hidden grin on the face of the shopkeeper.

"Yes," Earle said. "That's how the fish like them."

Back at the lake my husband pulled more gear out of the truck and loaded it into the boat: life preservers, fishing poles, crickets, assorted tackle boxes, a big basket that he told me is called a creel, bottled water, towels, and my sun hat. The boat had two swivel seats with armrests. I sat in back, and we motored onto the placid lake.

"This will do," he said as he guided the boat under some low-hanging branches and shut off the motor. "Now, I'll show you how to bait the hook." He handed me a pole, reached into the cricket cage, and pulled out a squiggly insect. He picked up his pole, found the hook, and neatly impaled the cricket, which continued to squirm.

"Now you try it," he said.

"You won't do it for me?" I said.

"Nope. You can do it. Just pass the hook through its body."

I was not expecting this. His eyes were on me. *He sees me as an equal and expects me to do it.* I moved into my objective clinical self as I reached into the cricket cage, caught one, brought it out, and stabbed the hook through its center. It squirmed. My clinical self suddenly disappeared.

"Earle, I feel like I can hear it screaming."

"It'll be fine, especially when you catch a fish," he said.

It did get better. I fed the fish a good many crickets. My hook came back with the insects nibbled off but no fish. Earle caught nine. Crappie, he said they were. Sort of like sunfish. They were small. I imagined that one played a game with me. I could see it just under the water from time to time, close to the boat. I kept casting my line right at it, but it never bit. I called it Moby Dick, and we laughed about that.

The hours of fishing were a meditation. We moved in and out of shadow, mostly drifting, water lapping softly at the sides of the boat. The sound became part of a symphony of birdsong, buzzing insects, and breezes playing gently in the trees. Colors were soothing greens, grays, pale yellow, and violet, with occasional flashes of sunlight that bounced off the water to dance on the soft underside of leaves. The scents of rotting vegetation, mud, and lake water were a fitting accompaniment. I felt folded into someplace deeply peaceful, lost in the rhythm of it. We did not talk much. We just fished. I felt incredibly connected to this man in his orange shorts and Kentucky-blue T-shirt and cap, beard now whiter than his still mostly brown hair. I had entered his world.

The sun rose higher, and Earle said, "It's time to go." He said fish won't bite when the sun warms the water. We returned to the boat ramp and reversed the process. This time Earle managed the maneuvering of the boat back onto the trailer as I packed up all the fishing gear. We both enjoyed the quiet as we set out for home. It felt very comfortable.

"You know," he said after a while. "When I'm out on the water I can forget everything. All the problems at work, all the worries. It all just disappears."

"I can understand that," I said. "It's a new experience for me. When I was little, maybe five or so, I used to go down to the creek with my dad while he fished from the bank. He loved it, too. I used to get worms out of the worm bucket for him. But being out there on the water is very different. It's soothing and peaceful."

Earle chuckled at my image, then returned to his own memories.

"I used to fish with Uncle Bud down at Gulf Shores in the summer. I really enjoyed that because dad was always working, it seemed. And then Larry and Jim and I used to motor over to H Lake in Arkansas whenever we could get away from the university. Oh, we had fun." Larry and Jim were longtime colleagues at the university in Memphis. I got to know them well when we lived there.

"I'm so glad we had today," I said.

"Me too, but just wait. More to come. We'll have fresh grilled fish tonight."

When we got home, Earle cleaned the nine little fish, grilled them, and the whole family enjoyed the bounty.

∽

There were some rough spots as we moved into that year.

"I don't know how you put up with me," I said one evening when Earle asked me to cook a meal that he liked, and I burst into tears. It suddenly felt like too much. "The Tamoxifen has done a number on me."

The drug I took to hold the cancer at bay had thrown me into early menopause. Some days I felt like an adolescent again—mood swings, crazy emotions popping up, hot flashes that drove me crazy. I couldn't sleep at night.

"Well, let's see," he said. "How many years do you have to take it?"

"Five years! But at least I don't need chemo."

"Well, only four and a half years left. That's the good news," he said with a grin.

"We can even buy an extra freezer for ice packs for your hot flashes."

"No more expenditures!" I said.

He laughed at that, and so did I.

That August, we decided to take a week for ourselves at a time-share we purchased in Lake Hamilton, Arkansas, during our early Memphis years. The children were all spending summer vacation with their other parent, giving us a spot of time.

The drive into Tennessee and through Memphis was a journey back in time. Sensory memories flooded back as we moved from the gentle hills of Kentucky onto flattening land. The green of late-summer foliage was intense and unrelenting. Long stretches of road were lined with trees wrapped in nets of kudzu, bent over into prehistoric shapes. As we approached Memphis, the flat Mississippi Delta, shaped by the river, spread out before us. I spotted the park just north of the city where Earle and I lunched that one day, and I remembered his strange and surprising request. It echoed in my head. *Will you help me die?*

As we moved closer to the edge of the city, I noticed smells that made my mouth water. Suddenly I wished we had time to stop for ribs at the Rendezvous restaurant, or a barbeque sandwich at Corky's. I wished we had time to spend an evening on Beale Street, visiting dark, smoky downstairs clubs where men and women sing the blues for the pure love of it, heads thrown back, lost in the joy. This city, which in many ways feels like a grown-up country town, saw me through so many major life changes in the ten years I lived there. The dissolution of a marriage, the formation of a new one, a graduate degree, job changes, blending families.

"Let's drive by our old house," I said.

"I was thinking the same thing," said Earle as he turned onto a street that would take us there.

"Interesting. It looks just the same, except for the neighborhood," I said.

"Yeah." He pointed down the street. "Look at all the businesses and the new apartment buildings. I think we moved just in time."

"I think we did too," I said.

We continued downtown toward the bridge, passing the University of Tennessee-Memphis, the Peabody Hotel, and the bright, shining building known as the Pyramid, a large multi-purpose structure on the edge of the river.

I remembered how I love the river. It had an energy that fascinated me.

"Do you remember when you brought me down here that day that I lost it?"

"Oh, do I," Earle said. "You were a mess. Do you remember the canoe race we entered during Memphis in May?"

"I do," I said. "That was so much fun even though we came in pretty much last. And I totally enjoyed John Denver's concert on Mud Island. I couldn't believe how long he performed. That was a special night for me."

We continued across the long span of bridge that took us into Arkansas and the flat, flat land that nourishes untold miles of rice paddies, silos popping up from time to time to hold the yield. Eventually, the road rose into the rolling hills around Hot Springs, and then our resort.

At last, relaxation. The resort was perched high on a hillside overlooking Lake Hamilton, rolling green hills behind it. Our unit overlooked the lake. We watched the sun set over the water in the evenings, boats gliding back to port and ducks hugging the shore looking for bits of crumbs. The ever-present bottle of wine sat on the table.

"I feel stuck," I mused one evening. "Surely there is more than this—work and survival?"

My thoughts drifted to things I used to enjoy. Reading, painting, taking walks, going to local horse events, dinners with friends. The things that nourished my soul. Activities somehow now forgotten. My experience with cancer was never really far from my mind. It was important now to take care of myself.

"Well," Earle said, "I do really miss tennis and the guys that I played with. This tennis elbow has totally destroyed my game. There is just too much pain to play."

I noticed the impact of the loss of that physical outlet. He was irritable at times with no way to channel the frustrations that came up about his work.

"There are rumbles again with my job." He poured another glass. "The chancellor is pushing me to look at doing more teaching. I don't know what's going on. Does he think I don't have enough to do? Do they really need someone else to teach in the clinical lab program? I could teach immunology for sure and would enjoy that, but another faculty member seems to have that sewed up. It's all a mystery. Makes me uneasy."

"Have you talked to the chancellor about that?"

"Well, not directly. I've been trying to understand his thinking. He's very evasive."

"Earle, that's not like you. You're not a person that has problems with directness as I see it. Just ask him."

"We'll see." He took another swallow.

I thought, *He has never been consistently settled and grounded in his work here. He tries to find enjoyment, as that is his nature, and there have been some good moments. But I remember the depth of his relationships with people at the university in Memphis and his enjoyment in his work there. I still wish that for him, but it seems like he doesn't have true backing from his superiors here.*

I was suddenly surprised by the thought: *Perhaps he is not able to do his job.* It sobered me.

I returned the conversation to my own train of thought, hoping for the kind of talks we used to have years ago.

"I really needed this time away," I said. "It feels so good to relax. I'm trying to let go of concerns about our financial situation and about Katie. You know, she just recently told me that she never told anyone about my surgery. Not even a school friend. She must have felt so alone in her worry."

"I did the best I could," he said, an edge of recrimination in his voice.

～

Things didn't feel right with Earle after we returned home. I was cooking dinner one evening, and he said from the living room, "I don't know why you didn't join a tennis league after your lessons. We could have had fun with that."

This was out of the blue.

"Earle, that was years ago. All of the league games for women are in the daytime, and I work. We talked about that."

"Well, we could have found some way. I think you don't want to do things with me."

I felt myself wanting to answer back, to argue. I was angry at his accusatory tone. It was unfair and unjustified. I stopped myself and continued cooking, leaving it. But the anger lingered.

This was so different from other times when he was very supportive. I felt off-balance.

As these rumblings happened, I was becoming increasingly aware that I was still me, but not the old me. I was changed by the life event of cancer and saw new things about myself. I felt at a point of putting things together differently, ideas about my work, my skills, my own values. It was a new way of being for me that grew out of an amazing gratitude for the gift of life.

Good things were happening with my teaching.

After dinner one night, I said, "I'm starting to see that I have value at work. It's a good feeling. Part of it is finally reaching a skill level with teaching that's allowing me to be more creative in the classroom. And part of it is getting positive comments from peers. But I'm struggling, too, with beginning to see the realities of academia. Politics are rampant."

"Oh, I sure know about that," he said with bitterness. "But I am truly glad for you."

~

The flowering crab on our front lawn was again in bloom, heralding a new spring. The additional tulip, hyacinth, and daffodil bulbs I planted the previous year filled the yard with color. It was now 1992. We took no pictures this year. We had only Katie still at home, and she was often off with friends. But she sought me out one day as I was drying the dishes.

"Mom, I need to tell you something. By trying to protect me from your cancer, you shut me out, and that made me feel even more alone."

I paused, wet dish in hand. Struck by her confession, I froze for a moment, the drips from the plate into the sink the only sounds. I inhaled deeply, set down the plate, dropped the damp towel onto the countertop, and turned to face my daughter. I didn't look her in the eye but stared at the floor as I recalled how I had curled inward during that time, directing all my energy, strength, and attention toward my healing. My hand went to my mouth as I responded. "Oh my . . . I can see that." I looked up. I saw *her*, in that moment. There was nothing to say except, simply, "I am so sorry I did that. Thank you for telling me." I reached out and hugged my daughter, her glossy dark hair soft against my cheek, grateful for her courage in taking the risk to speak her truth.

Then, suddenly, I saw that I had shut out a great deal of support for myself by thinking I could do it all. I did not even know how to ask.

~

I was in my fiftieth year. My youngest daughter, my last child, would be going to college in the fall, out of state, with the financial help of her father. I resigned from teaching and took a new job with the University of Kentucky rehabilitation program. It felt good to be back in clinical practice with a team of people that quickly came to feel like family. I allowed myself to get some help with cleaning the house, which gave some relief. Again, I turned to the question of what I wanted to do with the rest of my life. The responsibilities of children were no longer there. They were now on their own paths, independent of us. Space opened up to breathe, to think, to consider my own needs for nourishment and growth, long put on hold.

The first half of 1993 felt good. Earle was trying to help with finances by cutting back on his spending. He was again the Earle I knew, unconditionally loving. The man I fell in love with. His reassurance and caring helped shore me up when I felt stressed. After all I had endured with my health, I was still subject to struggles with body image and shifting hormones.

That June I received an unexpected gift. A dear bachelor uncle had passed away the year before. He left his nieces an inheritance of $30,000 each. The estate was settled, and I received a check. I felt enormous relief. Our house needed work, and I earmarked the money for a new roof, garage door, new kitchen floor, and redecorating of two rooms in the house. Before I had a chance to do any other planning, Earle laid claim to some of that money.

"I think we need to pay off my bills," he said and laid a few on the table in front of me.

I certainly knew about these, as I juggled with them every month.

I looked them over. "There are other things that need to be done, and there is not enough to pay off your bills."

He was not belligerent, but insistent.

It is time to be clear about my boundaries, I thought. *This is a gift to me, not him.*

I outlined the work that I wanted done on the house, said I wanted to give Michelle and Katie money toward a car, and after that, we would look at what might be left that could be applied to one or two of his bills. I did pay off two small bills of his and allowed myself about $200 for some new clothing. Then the money was gone.

※

Later in the summer, Mary and Katie stayed with us for a period of time before going back to college. One evening, they asked to sit down with me alone. I was puzzled but worked out some time.

"We're very worried about Earle," said Katie.

Surprised, I asked why.

"Mom, it's not normal for a man to put his fist through a screen door when he is mad about something."

"He's just been under a lot of job stress, actually for a long time, and it just got to be too much," I said.

"Mom. It's not normal. He needs counseling. He's drinking a lot too."

I knew exactly what they were talking about. On one occasion when all the girls were home at the same time, we had been having dinner. Something one of them said in casual conversation triggered him. He pushed back from the table, threw his chair against the wall, shouted in some very colorful language, and stormed out after punching at the screen door when it stuck, putting a hole through the screen. The outburst was unexpected, and I knew the girls were frightened. I had pushed this event away into those dark corners in my mind, along with numerous other instances of sudden outbursts.

My daughters were dead serious.

"OK. I'll talk with him."

I did talk with him, repeating the same words.

"It's not normal for someone to put his fist through a screen door in anger. You need to get some help to deal with your frustration."

"I was just angry that night, that's all."

I asked repeatedly about counseling. He never arranged it.

⁓

I came home early one day and found Earle also home, unusual for him. He was sitting on the bed in our bedroom, painted a soft sky-blue. His German shepherd, Willie, calmly rested his head on Earle's lap. Earle looked despondent.

"What's happened? You're home so early." I sat at the foot of the bed, faced him, and rested my hand on his leg.

"The chancellor has removed me from my position as vice-chancellor. He is going to move me into a full-time teaching position in my field with no change in salary or benefits. I guess I couldn't do the job as he saw it."

My heart dropped. I felt such pain for him. His dream for himself, gone.

"Oh, Earle. I am so, so sorry."

"Well, the good thing is we won't starve. I've still got a job and I'll just tell people I went back into the faculty."

"You know I'm here for you. We're in this together, like always," I said.

"I know."

I could only imagine what his feelings might be. Pain, hurt, betrayal, disappointment, feelings of failure. He never told me.

We saw the ad in a local arts newspaper we picked up in a coffee shop.

"Look at this," I said. "Imagine a church advertising in an arts magazine. I think that may be for us. And it's time to re-engage."

Earle agreed he'd like to get back into a church. We'd both backed away from one we'd been attending when church members were not supportive around the time of my surgery. We agreed we'd check out the Wednesday night service at this artsy church.

And so began our relationship with Church of the Resurrection, a small Episcopal church just outside of Lexington. We walked in the door, and it felt like home. The congregation was vibrant, active, young, and invested in each other. There were many avenues for involvement, and both of us found a place for ourselves. It provided spiritual nourishment within a welcoming community and became our spiritual home. As our children left, a place of spirit appeared for us.

One day, Earle came in the door with a large package under his arm.

"What do you have now?" I said, feeling a bit edgy.

With a beaming face, he opened up his treasure. Out came a complete chef's outfit, white jacket, apron, and a tall white hat.

"I need the right outfit for the Lobsterfest at the church. If I'm going to be cooking lobsters all day, I need the right clothing."

He should have been an actor. He was born for the stage.

This time, I found his excitement infectious. It was uncanny how he was able to experience joy in each adventure. Joining in at the lobster pot with the others, he just beamed, white hat standing out above the crowd.

My questions about understanding the path my life held for me were eased by the spiritual support I had found. Now it was 1994, and I had spent the past fourteen years with family, home, and work as my only focus. Both Earle and I were showing strains of living. I was having back issues, and both of us were diagnosed with diabetes. I was concerned about this as the disease is chronic, needing lifelong management. If we slipped into poor management, the long-term implications for health were serious.

Still, I began to feel as though I was being led. A painting class reignited my long-time interest in oil painting. It felt so good to reconnect with this way of self-expression. I felt a different kind of relationship growing with Earle but didn't yet see clearly what that would be. I wanted a change in our pattern of communicating, perhaps more honesty.

Then, in February 1995, my father died, which added to my reflections.

"Where do I go, what do I do?" became my guiding questions.

I reflected on my patterns of thinking. Almost everything I did was analytical. (The exception was my connection with my patients. That was intuitive and from the heart.) I was led back into my creative brain, finding writing similar to painting on a canvas. Words were brushstrokes. I worked at letting go of expectations that belonged to another time and place. I began to find an inner peace, feeling a guiding hand that was not mine. I heard, "Be still and pay attention." I saw myself touching other people.

We faced the empty nest and working, still struggling financially, but settled into a routine. Earle's wine consumption increased. Now he purchased it by the box.

One day, I received a letter from a colleague I had met during my teaching years at Eastern Kentucky University. She was now the chair of the Occupational Therapy Program at the University of Texas Health Science Center in San Antonio.

"Earle, I've been invited to apply for a position as coordinator for the development of a satellite Occupational Therapy Program at the University of Texas-Pan American in the Rio Grande Valley. I'm really flattered," I said. "But it's a big move. I'm not sure it's for me."

Over the next several days, we talked it through. I had not been looking for change. I was comfortable with my job and where we were in our lives. This would be a huge change. I couldn't tell whether I was more scared or excited.

Earle strongly pushed me to apply. "You have followed a man all of your working career. This is your time. Go for it."

My choice to go was about change and risk. On the surface, it was about work, but in truth, it was about the emergence of a self that had long been hidden away. The choice was about value, self-responsibility, and ownership of what I brought to those I touch.

I was grateful. My husband was a man who not only talked the talk but walked the walk. I was hired, and in March 1996, I moved to the Rio Grande Valley. We assumed Earle would find work there quickly, given his long and successful university and teaching history. That was not to be the case.

CHAPTER 6

A Healing Path

As a wife, I could tell you about the ways I weaved my life with my husband's and he weaved his life with mine, and I could leave it at that. But I could also tell you about another thread that pulled me through. I can see that it began in October 1990, when I faced breast cancer; it was a month that fell into the middle of the most difficult decade of my life.

Ten years before, when I met this man who awakened me to a new life, we were entering the prime of our lives. We were young, eager, vibrant, holding in our minds a shared dream of a life of personal and professional fulfillment. There were no unplanned events in this dream, only the wish to gently grow old together, enjoying our remaining years.

This thread first appeared as a strand to be woven, in Dr. K's office where I waited for the pre-op visit for my mastectomy. I sat there, muscles tight, anxious, scared, not quite panicked but close. His office, decorated in muted colors in the neutral way of all doctor's offices, without personality, allowed me to create my own story, one filled with fears.

He walked in, a slight, pleasant-looking man. I liked that he sat down in the armchair near me. He began to give basic information about how the day of the surgery would go, what I could expect during the check-in procedure, and so on. I interrupted, peppering him with anxiety-driven questions and concerns. They burst out of me. I wanted to know all the details about what would follow, how soon could I go home, what would I be able to do, and so on. He stopped me.

"Don't jump ahead," he said. "Simply take each day and event as it comes."

His message was simple. Stay in the present. But it was the emotional support I felt from him that made it powerful. He was fully present, not distracted, not reading notes, not talking about statistics. He was just there. A positive, caring presence, talking just to me. I could not name it then, but he was teaching me.

If I were asked to identify a time when the concept of healing came into my awareness, I'm not sure I could. I remember being fascinated by the *Natural History* magazine subscription my mother began for me when I was about nine or ten. I raced to the articles about indigenous peoples and their beliefs and healing practices. Later, when I chose my career, I was drawn to a health-care profession: occupational therapy. During my years of practice, I was continually amazed by the miracle of our bodies, how, despite horrendous injury and the devastation of disease, the body somehow knew how to heal.

My studies in neurology and neuroanatomy brought understanding of how our sensory systems give us information about our outer and inner worlds. I was most interested in the power of touch; I gave presentations to health-care personnel, including physicians, as to the importance of touch, especially with geriatric clients.

As the chair of the Occupational Therapy Program at the University of Texas-Pan American, I was responsible for purchasing cadavers for our gross anatomy course and overseeing the dissection labs. Again, I was in awe of the miracle of the human body and felt that the learning provided by those who donated their bodies was not only scientific but spiritual.

But if I were asked to identify the specific moment in time when I understood healing in a most intimate and personal way, the origin was breast cancer.

～

Four days after the surgery, while I was still in the hospital, Dr. K walked into my room, took my hand, and smiled into my eyes.

"I wanted to let you know all looks good," he said. "We got all of the cancer, and based on the report, you are just a shade into stage two and will most probably just need to take a preventive medication. I'm going to send you to an oncologist for follow-up."

Simple words, clear information, the touch of a hand, and a smile. The words gave me enormous relief. His touch and his smile gave me hope.

～

Dr. H did the reconstruction immediately following the mastectomy. He was a gentle, soft-spoken man, very deliberate in all that he did. His pace was his own and he could not be rushed by any hospital policy. Late at night, after the surgery, the nurses paged him to come to my room.

"What is the matter?" he asked with concern.

"I'm in so much pain I can barely breathe," I said, my body almost rigid with the effort of not moving. I still had the nasogastric tube, the catheter, the IVs, the drains in my chest, and the fog of anesthesia. In my hand I held a small plastic plunger, the precious deliverer of morphine. I was afraid to use it. In my scrambled state, I was afraid I would overdose.

Dr. H leaned over the bed rail and gently brushed my bangs away from my forehead. It felt like a mother's touch; comforting, caring. He did not rush. His touch brought me into focus, allowed me to hear.

"I'll have the pharmacist come to see how we can help you," he said. "And we'll take the tube out of your nose in the morning. It's there only in case you become nauseated by the anesthesia." He smiled, then said everything was as it should be.

The pharmacist appeared quickly and gave me an injection to ease the pain. He also explained that there was no way to overdose with the morphine as the machine automatically prevented that from happening. I felt relieved.

A few days later I was feeling well enough to brush my hair and put on some lipstick. Dr. H came into the room, making rounds, and his face burst into a big smile.

"I see you're feeling better. You're looking much better."

"I do feel better," I said, glowing inside that someone had noticed.

Earle had been coming by every day after work, caring, but often still tied to events of his day.

My relationship with Dr. H continued for several months as close follow-up was necessary. I said to him on one visit, "You're not like other physicians. I can't put my finger on it, but there is something about the way you handle things that is different."

"I'm from Ecuador," he said. "That is where I got my basic medical education. In my country, we do not have all of the modern technology that exists here, and so we learn other ways to help people heal."

👁 👁 👁

We learn other ways to help people heal. That simple statement was profound for me. I felt like it entered me and pulled together a lifetime of threads that had been looking for the garment they would form. *I have been a good occupational therapist for almost twenty-five years, but I have not been a healer.* A beginning awareness. A first step on a new path. I began finding and reading books that were guideposts for understanding what healing was and how that fit with my current awareness. I read books on healthy ways to deal with stress, on resilience after trauma, and on mind-body medicine. Scientists were defining links between the power of belief systems and health, and the relationship between our biochemistry and health. I read everything I could find. It was a new world of learning.

At first, the journey on my healing path was about increased awareness of my changing perceptions. Learning from my physician teachers, I paid more attention to the power of words to evoke emotions or to calm and soothe. I listened to how people used words. I paid more attention to how I used words and how many I used. I began to see that often my saying less allowed the other person space to share more.

After leaving teaching in 1992 to return to clinical practice at the University of Kentucky rehabilitation department, feedback from some patients suggested something about me had begun to change. One geriatric client told me, "When I come to see you, I feel peace."

I was moved. I wondered what had prompted him to say it. Then I realized that I felt peace when I was working with him. Where did that come from, I wondered?

There were others who touched me, who I later wrote about in *OT Practice* magazine, the trade publication for the American Occupational Therapy Association.[1]

A young police officer, Tim, who had been shot in the hand at a routine traffic stop, talked about being torn between wanting to return to work while his family was asking him to find another job. He told me that I kept him in present time and that it was the caring that mattered most. He told me that he felt that I was the only person who listened.

I remember Arthur as well. He was a man whose hand was amputated in a sawmill accident, then reattached. His wife told me that it was my encouragement, joking, and inclusion of his family that fostered trust. She said I let him tell his story. The injury was not only about him. It was about the whole family.

A middle-aged woman, Rosie, who suffered a partial amputation of her hand at the wrist when an O-ring machine malfunctioned, told me that the hope I offered kept her going and gave her the time to gather enough emotional and physical strength to take on her new reality. Her family members were struggling with their own emotions and were not able to support her.

My patients were teaching me.

A transformation was taking place. I came to see my cancer as a gift that led me into a much deeper and very personal understanding of healing. My readings on the subject of healing and my life teachers, which included my patients, were allowing me to see that my way of relating had changed. I was no longer focused only on technique and treatment plans. I was now focused on the people, their stories, and their spirits. When I met a patient for the first time, the first thing I tried to find was their spirit. I found it in their eyes, their voice, and in what they gave back to me.

◎ ◎ ◎

This woman who was awake and alive and coming into new awareness about healing was the woman who would arrive in Edinburg, Texas, in March 1996. Not the woman who, for many years, saw no way forward for herself.

"Why don't we just pack as much into the car as we can, and drive down," Earle said. "I can take a few days from work and do that."

I was grateful for his offer and agreed. What we brought in the car was what I started out with, in a furnished apartment that Bruce, one of the college faculty members, had helped us find. I settled into it as a temporary residence. I wanted it to be very temporary as the walls were pea green and the furniture was brown vintage Goodwill. We had sold our house in Lexington, and the plan was for Earle to handle the details of closing and then move into a furnished apartment there until he found a job in Texas. After he was sure I was settled, he drove back to Lexington. We both hoped that the time apart would be short. He had already begun to research possible openings in the higher education systems in the Rio Grande Valley that would fit his skills. We phoned every evening. The calls kept us connected.

By early summer of 1996, I was settled in a duplex in neighboring McAllen, and with the addition of an excellent secretary and the hiring of another faculty member, we were ready for the first class of students. One afternoon in June, I found a mailing announcing a three-day event in Corpus Christi, Texas: X International Congress of Traditional and Folk Medicine. Corpus was only a two-and-a-half-hour drive. I received approval from the university to attend the workshop and on a warm June day, I drove to Corpus Christi and pulled into the convention center parking lot just in time for the opening.

It began with a sound that sent chills through me. Mayan healers and holy men processed into the arena of the convention center to open the conference. Wearing red robes with gold trim and elaborate headdresses, the men carried bowls of copal, a smoky, faintly pine-scented incense. I took in the smell and smoke as it permeated the air. I looked for the source of the sound: It was coming from the blowing of conch shells. I felt it, a calling of ancestors, supernaturals, blessings, mysticism, and magic. The march was slow and deliberate as they created a ring around the floor of the arena, then stopped. Except for a single man who chanted, the arena fell quiet. I felt enveloped by spirit. Every person was wrapped in the spell. I was experiencing the creation of sacred space.

The range of healing practices and the traditions of healers who presented workshops amazed me. Dr. H's words echoed in my head as I listened to shamans, dream-workers, and other holy men and women. One workshop was about *curanderismo*, a healing practice not only for physical illnesses but for illnesses of soul and spirit. The woman presenting explained that curanderismo grew out of rural Mexico and Guatemala and still existed in practice in the culture in which I now lived, which was 88 percent Hispanic. I was learning other ways to help people heal.

On our first Thanksgiving apart, I flew back to Lexington to be with my husband. Months had gone by and Earle had sent out letters of inquiry regarding administrative positions. There were responses, but so far, no conclusive forward movement. He had handled the closing on our house and was now in his furnished apartment. We had much to catch up on. I had so much I wanted to tell him about my new job, my discoveries, the traditional medicine conference, the people I was meeting, and my new students. I wanted to include him in my life as fully as I could. We talked for long hours, filling each other in. He talked about his teaching assignments in the department of clinical lab sciences.

"The coursework is so familiar," he said. "Having worked my way through graduate school as a medical technologist allows me to weave in real-life examples. The students seem to enjoy that, and I certainly do."

I was happy for him. He was doing what he knew he did well and was respected by his colleagues and students.

The next morning, he said, "I want to show you something. Come on outside."

It was a cold, blustery day. Dark clouds hinting of snow billowed across the sky. He led me out into the parking lot to a shape covered with a black tarp, which he pulled off with a flourish. There stood an emerald-green Kawasaki motorcycle. I was speechless. I knew he'd had a motorcycle when he was younger. I knew he had sold it after he had an accident. I knew that he had enjoyed it. But all I could think of was the cost. He didn't seem to notice that I didn't exclaim with joy. He didn't seem to notice my clenched hands.

"I've been wanting another motorcycle for a long time," he said. "It is such a smooth ride and will save gas money because I'll ride it to work. It's called a Nomad. Maybe you can get one too."

His excitement was palpable. A new machine. He had started letting his hair grow long in anticipation of the ponytail he had been talking about for some months. It was what motorcyclists wore.

Well, he's alone in this rented apartment and has gone through a change at work. I can see how he would need some distraction. But at the same time, something shifted in me, and I decided it was time to take his name off the credit cards.

On my flight back to the Rio Grande Valley, the thought of the ponytail triggered an insight. Earle's creativity allowed him to incorporate new learning almost immediately in his teaching. He had a knack for turning incoming information into coherent streams going out, in a fully integrated package. His eagerness for new ideas included incorporating new personas, along with creative costumes. I suddenly realized that there was nothing contradictory about his ponytail. He was changing personas—from university administrator to faculty.

My perceptions were changing too. I was on a plane headed back to Texas, leaving my husband in Lexington. I was alone. I knew people at work but had not yet developed close friendships. Thoughts about my mother surfaced. My mother, one of seven children, was a first-generation American who lived through the Great Depression. When she graduated from high school, she was offered a scholarship to college, but the family needed her income and she had to turn it down. Her world was church and family. An older sister died of tuberculosis at eighteen. A pair of twin siblings was stillborn, and the last to be born died of an unknown event at age two. It was not an era of sharing feelings or exploring the self. It was an era of survival. As an adult she had friends but shared her difficulties and her struggles only with my sister and myself. My father had been diagnosed with Parkinson's disease as a relatively young man, and as his disease slowly progressed, she leaned more and more on the two of us to talk through her feelings, her complaints, her own illnesses. My sister and I came to feel her needs as a burden. We tried to support her, but it was as if she just needed to talk and was not able to hear and use what we offered.

"Mom, you've got to talk to others about things that bother you," I would say. "You have a lot of friends here. They'd be able to support you. Jane and I are so far away now."

"We keep things in the family," she said firmly, as always.

I saw the cost to her in stress-related illnesses later in her life. I saw similarity in my inability to share with anyone during the Lexington years. As I flew back to Texas, my place of new beginnings, I set a clear goal for myself. *I want to learn how to build a support system for myself.* I visualized this community as a group of women able to share on a deep and personal level, much as I had found in the cancer support group I attended for three years. I wasn't sure how that would unfold but I knew, for my emotional health, I would need the support of others.

I needed a home—a church home. I found that in St. Matthew's Episcopal Church in Edinburg. I liked that it was a small congregation, even though there were larger Episcopal churches in the area. Perhaps thirty-five people made up the Sunday morning service, and there were Hispanics as well as Anglos worshipping together. People were friendly, and I soon began to feel anchored.

Sally was my first friend there, a bubbly, adventure-loving person. One day after church, she came up to me waving a blue flyer in my face.

"Judy, Judy, you've got to go to this," she said, handing it to me. The flyer announced a Healing Touch Level I workshop in San Antonio. I read through the material and was interested. I knew nothing about the program, but the content revolved around energy and specific healing techniques. I wanted to learn more.

I enjoyed how good it felt to just be able to make my own decisions as I drove the four hours north to San Antonio. I didn't have to consult with anyone or worry about having to get back to prepare a meal. I missed Earle, and we debriefed every night by phone, but the experience of new freedoms was exhilarating. Even the freedom to work as hard as I was working, often through the weekends, was my choice.

My first Healing Touch training of fifteen hours was spread out over Friday evening, Saturday, and Sunday. The program had been developed by Janet Mentgen, a nurse, in 1980. Others joined in her efforts over the next several years and established a structured series of workshops with a curriculum eventually leading to certification.

A dozen people were in my group. We sat in a circle in a large room with massage tables behind us.

In a friendly and caring but professional way, our instructor began to explain:

"Within this workshop, you'll learn about the human energy system and its relationship to physical, emotional, mental, and spiritual health. You will also learn energy principles basic to Healing Touch. You'll learn how to do an assessment and will have learned fifteen specific healing techniques by the end of the weekend."

I felt a little overwhelmed but excited too. I noticed both emotions at work in me.

After short lectures, we practiced with partners to try out what we had learned. I connected easily. *So that's what energy feels like.* As I moved my hands, held about an inch or so from my partner's body, slowly from head to toe, I could feel temperature changes, sometimes warm, sometimes hot, and sometimes cool. Each person had a different pattern. What allowed this awareness was the very first thing we learned: centering.

"Centering is about being fully present, focused, and open to guidance," the instructor said. "The goal is to connect deeply with your inner self, without ego, which allows connection to a higher power, in order to be fully present and open to the person you are working with."

We used a centering meditation and practiced on each other for a whole morning. I noticed that as I became still and open inside, I was able to experience the energy of the other person without even trying.

During that first workshop, I learned about chakras and meridians, as well as the fifteen techniques. Our instructor also stressed that what was equally important was self-growth and self-care. "It is important to take care of yourselves."

How empowering it was for me to hear that message. A permission and an affirmation.

꧁꧂

I hadn't seen my friend Barb for years. She was one of my classmates in the Occupational Therapy Program, and we had become close, staying connected despite distance. I got a call one day, saying she was having a rough time and wanted to visit. We worked that out and I picked her up at the Corpus Christi airport during Easter week. As we loaded her bag into the car and started the drive to my home, I could see the tension in her busyness and hear the anxiety in the pitch of her voice. She had been through a lot, and I knew she was strong. But at the moment she seemed to have forgotten that.

Some days after we settled in, I suggested a Healing Touch technique to help her relax. I still felt fairly new at it but believed in its power. She agreed. I set up my bedroom in the back of the house, leaving only a dim light on. The scent of candles, vanilla and desert rose, filled the room. Calming meditation music drifted in. Barb lay down on the bed, feet up on the pillow, head at the foot. I sat behind her head.

The technique involved a series of ten light finger placements on neck, head, and face, each held for several minutes, or until the energy flow felt balanced. I prepared myself. I imagined myself grounded, rooted to the earth. When I felt that solidity, I let the light come. It came from some place above, from the limitless beyond, and flowed into the top of my head and down my spine and then up to my shoulders, through my arms to my hands.

I became a channel for that flow of light and began the series of finger placements. My mind held nothing but awareness of the light flowing through me toward this person who was troubled. The loving flow was that of divine energy. I was aware of the music and the scent of the candles intermingling with the light, and it felt as though I was holding a golden glow. I moved slowly through all of the hand placements, and when I was through, I told Barb she could lie there as long as she liked. Then I left the room.

Later, she emerged from the bedroom with tears running down her face, her eyes red. She came and sat next to me on the couch. I put my arm around her and waited.

"I felt so loved. I felt so loved," she said, tears and choked sobs still coming.

"You are," I said. "You are," still feeling the light with me.

We sat for a while. She slowly stopped crying and then quietly started talking, relaxed now and calm.

"I felt like I left my body for a while. I was beside the bed, seeing us, but I was dancing with the music, whirling and spinning. Like a blur. Then I was kneeling beside the bed. I was a little child, my elbows on the edge, just watching."

I accepted these words with no comment other than a soft, "That's interesting."

We visited and talked, and just like that, it was time for her to leave. She had found her strength again. I saw it in her eyes and heard it in her voice as we hugged for a last time, murmuring our goodbyes.

~

On the phone, I tried to explain to Earle what the Healing Touch workshop was like: how moved I felt at the power of this way of working. I felt him listening attentively, though we were miles apart.

"I'm pleased you found that program," he said, and the energy behind his words sounded genuine. "It sounds like it fits your interests, and I totally support you doing this."

On Christmas break, he traveled to see me in the Rio Grande Valley. We had three weeks to be together. It felt like a luxury. There was actually time to talk, the way we used to talk. I hoped our retirement would be this way.

Right off, I told him about my mother, who had just had another heart attack the day before. "I feel so down. It's hard not to be there, but the distance is huge, and I'm tied into my work."

"Tell me about it," he said. "This has happened before, and she's pulled through. What do you know?"

He listened as I filled him in on the details. "The prognosis is good. She is stable."

"Your mother is a tough, strong-minded woman," he said. "Sounds like she'll be back home in no time." His arm went around me, and we sat in quiet for a bit. Then we went on to other things. He seemed to have a need to talk.

"I've been reading a lot of interesting books," he said. "One of them really speaks to me about how I need to look under the hood at my own needs, to learn about what my own needs are. When you had cancer, I was so afraid I would lose you. I need you so much to balance the life I live, mostly in excess."

"I never knew you were afraid," I said. "What I felt was your total support. You were my strength."

I snuggled into his arm, against his chest, feeling the warmth of him, smelling the scent of him as we sat together on our couch, enjoying the last mellowing rays of the tropical sun. Much later that night, as I was in that twilight zone before sleep overtakes, I found myself with a new awareness of him, hearing him say how much I meant to him. I was touched.

A few days later, sitting outside on the back porch in the cooling air that was coming in off the Gulf, I brought up another thought. "I've been reviewing my journal," I said. "It helps me to do that from time to time to find perspective, and I was reminded how hard things have been for us, for a lot of years."

"I could never have survived it without you," he said. "That's why I want you to have this time."

I felt as though he knew on some level what the cost had been for me.

"Just a minute. I have something I want to give you," he said. He disappeared inside, then shortly reappeared with a rolled-up scroll. Surprised, I unrolled it. It was a certificate for a series of ten writing classes with a well-known author in my town.

"I'm so touched, Earle," I said. "How did you make this happen? How did you find her?" I had talked about this course when he first came. I wanted so much to do it, but money was tight, and I did not feel I could add that expense.

"I saw how much it meant to you, so I just asked around town and did my research." His face was one big smile. "You work so hard and never give yourself the things that nourish you. I want you to have this."

I did not know then, but this gift would lead me into a writing group where I found new learning and friendships that became a bedrock of support and encouragement for the next ten years of my life. I had found a new way of expression that met a need in me that I did not know I had until I began writing.

It seemed time to look for a house. We decided it made sense to funnel the rental money into a home. My job was secure, and Earle was still looking for work. Eventually, we would need an anchor. As we talked through our financial resources, I told him about a decision I had made.

"I've taken your name off the credit cards I'm using here in Texas. I would like you to go ahead and take my name off any that you are using in Lexington."

He looked surprised but agreed.

"It's a way to keep our finances uncomplicated," I said. "We live in two different states, and now we have two different bank accounts. Just makes sense to me."

For some reason, I didn't tell him that I had been slowly paying off my cards.

In early spring, I started looking at homes and eventually found one that would be a direct purchase from the owner. It was small, on a quiet street, not far from campus. I liked the fenced-in yard. It would hold our dogs. I also loved the ruby red grapefruit tree and the lemon tree in the back yard. I saw the possibility for my own private space in the tool shed out back. Earle flew down to see it and met the present owners. He approved. It felt good to finally know we would soon be in a home.

Earle returned to Lexington, and I began the process of managing the purchase. We would be approved for the mortgage with five percent down. I called Earle, excited.

"We're ready. All I need is for you to mail me a check for the $8,000 we made on the sale of the Lexington house and we can move ahead."

A pause. "It's gone," he said.

"What?"

Every fiber of my being came to a standstill. I stood, holding the phone to my ear, frozen in shock and disbelief. Emotions crashed. I was crashing.

"What? What do you mean it's gone?"

"Well, I needed things."

I remembered the motorcycle, the new electronics that filled his furnished apartment. I searched in my mind to remember more. It seemed like there must have been more. Suddenly, his apartment seemed light-years away.

"I can't believe you did that!" I shouted into the phone. "That was our nest egg."

I was furious. No, heartbroken.

"How are we going to buy a house? I can't talk to you now." I hung up.

I sobbed. This was betrayal. I felt so, so angry. Most of my inheritance from my uncle had gone into that house, and now it was gone.

My community of women was not yet developed, so I called my sister and spent a long time on the phone sobbing. She was furious, too, adding many unkind comments about Earle. It was so helpful to have her support right then. We were very different, just wired differently, and had not been close for a while. Her unflinching support of me in a time of agonizing pain was more than I could have hoped for and gave me strength. In that terrible valley, something hardened in me. It was a cold, bleak awareness that I was on my own financially. I had to assume full responsibility for our financial path and could no longer depend on Earle.

In the next days, I talked with the owner of the house about how to manage the purchase.

"Well, you can perhaps get a loan from people you know," he said.

And that is what I did. The whole business was touchy because banks will not accept a loan as a down payment. The money must be given as a gift.

I felt demeaned, embarrassed. I was a fifty-seven-year-old woman who went to her mother and sister for a donation to make up a down payment on a house because her husband, a sixty-year-old man, had squandered their scarce resources. My sister knew the reason and was not pleased with the request, but she came through. I did not tell my mother why we needed the help. I just said it had been a financial strain to live apart. She was quick to send the money. Both had to declare the donation a gift.

I bought the house in my name and paid them both back over time out of my salary. Earle and I never discussed his use of the money or my reaction to it. I never knew how he felt about what had happened. Somewhere inside, I just took control and charged ahead. I could not reopen that wound.

By April of 1998, I had moved in. It felt good to be in a home. The process helped me feel grounded, and I enjoyed creating my own space. I sent Earle pictures, and our evening phone calls included updates on where I had put furniture and the few belongings I had. I did look forward to him joining me there. He was thinking about taking early retirement so he could move forward with his life.

※

The two years apart had been more difficult for Earle than for me. I was perpetually busy with the developing program, immersed in my own growing and learning. For me, it felt like the hardest but most creative time of my professional life. But I was aware of how different it was for Earle. He had responded to job opportunities at two universities in the Rio Grande Valley and one in San Antonio. He was interviewed at all three places and was a semifinalist in each situation. He went into each interview with hope and energy, seeing all that he could contribute, and rightly so, but was not chosen. It was very hard for me to see him disappointed again and again, and to hear the mood swings from hope and excitement to loss. I felt torn by that. Many times, I questioned whether I should just resign and go back to Lexington. I felt that conflict within me, always there: my need or his need.

In May, there was a Level II: A Healing Touch workshop scheduled in Austin, this time in the home of one of the class assistants. Sally and I went together. In this workshop, the goals included further development of higher sense perception, working with spiritual guidance, self-healing, and self-development, as well as advanced techniques. The format was the same. We practiced on each other. We gave and received. It was a time of deep healing for me. I felt the energy from my partner as she allowed the flow, given in love. The experience was one of deep relaxation beyond the simple relaxations of massage or reading a really good book. Something happened on a cellular level that allowed connections within me, affecting every part of my being. By the end of the fifteen-hour program, I felt restored and at peace. There was healing for my anger and rest for my soul.

Earle would begin early retirement in June, bringing the rest of the furniture and his belongings to Texas in a U-Haul. A group of friends from our Lexington church helped him pack up his apartment, and he hired a group of workers to help him load the truck. He asked if I would fly up and drive back to Texas with him, and I agreed.

One evening on the phone, he said, "I've been thinking about something I'd like to do."

I waited.

"My retirement plan from the University of Kentucky has a cash option," he said. "I want to withdraw as much money as we need to pay off all of our debts. I am willing to do that. I could take care of everything but the mortgage and the car payment."

Reparation.

I was floored. I didn't know whether to laugh or cry or shout for joy. I allowed my heart to soften, open enough to remember that despite all the difficulties of the past two years, he was at heart a generous and caring man. I could feel the unraveling of the months and years of tension in my body. What emerged was a glimmer of hope. Hope that we could move into retirement years in a way that would nourish us both. We had both worked hard all of our lives, and my wish for retirement was to be able to travel, paint, write, and just have time to *be*, knowing that we were financially secure. Earle's wishes were for time to fish, perhaps to sail, to enjoy being near water. I felt that there was potential for us to manage this scenario.

CHAPTER 7

All Was Not As We Had Dreamed

The sound of hammering rang across the yard as transformation of the tool shed into my healing room began. I stood and watched as two men worked on the white frame building set on a concrete slab, on the right side of the yard about twenty feet from the house and perpendicular to it. The room that would become my healing room was fifteen by ten feet, had a heavy wooden sliding door on the front and a window on each end. The roof overhung the front, allowing a porch wide enough to hold a folding chair or two. Our plan was to replace the wooden door with a sliding glass patio door, add two more windows on the back side, install a small air conditioning-heater combo, then insulate, put up wallboard, and lay carpet. All that was work to be done by others. My joy would be to paint and furnish.

☙ ☙ ☙

It was a huge relief. The decision Earle made to withdraw money from his retirement to pay off all of our debts was pivotal. For almost the first time in our marriage, I felt like I could breathe. With the absence of bills, some money freed up. We decided to do two things. One was to turn the tool shed into a place just for me. Our house was small, and Earle seemed to fill all the space in whichever room he was sitting. He was a big man, over two hundred twenty-five pounds. Gadgets always seemed to surround him, and his hearing was failing. Either music or TV was turned to a higher volume than I appreciated. The living room and small dining area were connected, and the galley kitchen had a window in the wall over the sink that looked out into the living room. If my husband was in any one of these areas, he was in view. The house had three bedrooms, the smallest of which Earle identified as his office. One I wanted as a guest room, and the master bedroom had room only for our bed and two dressers. A bathroom opened off of that bedroom, and I declared that as mine; the large bathroom off the hall became Earle's.

"I need a space," I said. "I need a place to start seeing Healing Touch clients, to paint, to write, to journal, and to work on preparation for my classes. A place where I can just think."

"Well then," Earle said. "We need to make sure it's done well and includes everything you need." He jumped into the project with gusto and made many good suggestions. I felt we were working as a team. It was a good feeling and brought back memories of the connections we shared in the first years of knowing each other. The feeling never changed for me. We were bound energetically. We were meant to be together. It began with a moment in a classroom, twenty years ago, when I somehow knew we would be married. I saw now that Earle's request on that fall day in a park, asking if I would help him die, was not about a wondering thought but about a connection of energy that was not of our conscious choosing. In the lightning storms of hard times, the light sputtered but always came back on, reminding me to trust.

☙

The second decision was to invite all of our children to our home for Christmas 1998. We could afford to pay their airfare, and the last time we had all been together was in 1995, when my older daughter, Mary, got married to Chris in Memphis.

It proved to be a most interesting Christmas. Mary and Chris, Mark, Michelle, and Katie all flew in about the same time. We found nearby motel rooms for some of them, as our house was so small. We gave Earle's truck to Mark to use so he could act as a taxi service, and everyone gathered at the house for meals and for Christmas gift-giving. I was so happy to see them all.

But something was awry. Earle used the festive occasion as a reason to not only have wine always available but margaritas as well. His drinking started in the afternoons, and his mood became foul. He sat in his recliner in the living room with a surly expression as happy chatter went on around him. Mary and Michelle were joking with each other, and Earle suddenly lashed out at them. "Stop being bitches," he said. This drew stunned silence. He was more than unpleasant. He was an ass. Everyone either left the room or withdrew into himself or herself.

I saw what was happening. He was expecting to be the center. He was expecting everyone to sit around him and listen to his stories. But what happened instead was these young people were so excited to see each other that they became their own group. They got along well and had great fun together with laughter, teasing, and joking. I was surprised to discover that there was a part of me that also wanted to be the center.

It's not that I didn't feel the pull of Earle's dark mood, but I stepped back and looked at the whole scene, and I thought, *I want to be part of the group that's having fun.* And that's what I did. We allowed Earle to go his own way emotionally. He isolated himself, was grumpy and asocial.

The highpoint of the holidays was a trip to South Padre Island, a lovely beach about eighty-five miles from our house. Even in December, it was warm enough to play in the water, chase seagulls, and enjoy the absolute beauty of the place. In the evening, the young people took over the kitchen, Chris and Mark taking the lead, and prepared a wonderful seafood dinner.

In the aftermath of goodbye hugs, Earle and I settled down to rest and debrief, me in my cozy upholstered chair and Earle in his recliner. The dogs lazed in the sun pouring in through the sliding glass door.

"Well, that was an interesting visit," my husband said.

"What do you mean?" I said.

All Was Not As We Had Dreamed

"Chris certainly seemed to think he knew a lot about a lot of things."

"Oh," I said. "Do you mean about the computer?" Chris and Earle had gotten into a lengthy discussion about some computer issue. "Well, that's his field," I said.

"Everyone just seemed to do their own thing," he said. "I didn't feel like they connected with me."

"Earle, you isolated yourself, were cranky most of the time, and you were drinking an awful lot. Not a good formula for connection."

"I'm still recovering from the radiation," he said. "I've done nothing but sit for the last two months."

It was clear to me that his endurance was poor. He spent those months of recovery watching old westerns, then drifting into naps. He did not look well.

"I know it's been hard," I said. "But I think the worst is over."

Bruce, who was then the chair of one of the departments in the college of allied health, was one of the first people I met when I moved to Edinburg. In fact, he had helped me find my first apartment—the one with the pea-green walls.

He and Earle had hit it off and become fast friends when Earle joined me in 1998. Bruce's wife, Joan, was equally as welcoming. We visited each other's homes and socialized together. Bruce and Earle shared an enjoyment of good beer and football, as well as endless discussions about the politics of academia. Bruce offered Earle his first faculty appointment, teaching several sections of medical terminology.

I was glad Earle had the teaching assignment, which spanned January to May of 1999. It lifted his spirits. During the recovery from the radiation, his mood had been changeable, and I never knew what to expect when I got home. It seemed like the beginning of a downhill slide, and I was the one on whom he leaned. He was eager to become part of St. Matthew's, but often his unpredictable bladder kept him at home. As we moved into the new year that situation improved, and he quickly made friends at the church. He was gregarious, warm, and responsive. He drew people to him. He joined Education for Ministry (EFM), an educational program in the Episcopal Church that meets nine months out of the year for four years. It is an education in church history but also in spiritual self-exploration. He loved the program and urged me to join, but I was feeling overwhelmed at work.

At St. Matthew's, he was known by some as a big teddy bear. His gusto for all things included music. He had brought two guitars with him into our marriage, and he occasionally got them out and played and sang. There was a particular hymn in church that seemed to bring something out in him that he could not suppress. The hymn, sometimes used during Communion was "I Am the Bread of Life." He loved it and entered in with his full baritone. He was never concerned about hitting the right note. It was about the message. The refrain always led to his arms raised up to the heavens. I found myself doing the same. He lived his present moment and was unconcerned about others in the congregation who might be a little more restrained.

He also developed new friendships in the motorcycle community as he tooled around town on his Nomad.

I was very ready for his increased independence because my workload remained heavy. New faculty were added. I was teaching a full course load as well as handling the administrative issues of the program. As a department, we were preparing for transition from a satellite program of the Health Science Center San Antonio to an independent, freestanding program at the University of Texas-Pan American. This required a significant amount of negotiation between the two universities and the accreditation arm of the American Occupational Therapy Association. Part of the accreditation process required the completion of a yearlong self-study of the existing program. It was a herculean, analytical, and highly detailed process and all faculty were required to take part. After that was completed, there was an on-site visit of three days in which a team examined all areas of the document submitted. The pressure was intense. It felt never-ending.

Earle was aware of this. When I went through a rough patch, I would come home and find a beautiful bouquet of flowers waiting for me on the dining table.

"I thought you might need these," he'd say, smiling. And I did.

I did join him in Leadership Edinburg, a program to introduce newcomers to the community. It was actually very interesting and not as time-consuming as EFM would have been for me. I enjoyed it.

Eventually, the work on my healing room was finished. Now I could paint and furnish. I chose a pale, soft blue color for the walls and moved in a solid brown desk, placing it under the end window that looked down the strip of lawn at the side of our house. A filing cabinet and a tall, narrow bookshelf that Earle's father had made flanked either side of the desk. I had purchased a teal massage table a month earlier and, when collapsed, it fit nicely under a back-facing window. My grandmother's secretary, the varnish now aged and dark, fit between the two back windows. I had always considered it special because it reminded me of a family story. My maternal grandfather had given it to my grandmother, Nanny, as a wedding gift and it found its place in their bedroom. Nanny was my favorite grandmother. She lived three houses away and was an unconditionally loving presence in my life. This old piece of furniture connected me to her and brought her into my healing space. With this in place, there was just enough room left for a rocking chair purchased from Mast general store in Boone, North Carolina, where Katie had gone to college, and another small bookcase. Big beige and blue pillows lay scattered on the floor.

I hung light, creamy curtains over the bottom half of the windows and placed paintings and objects that were special to me on the walls. The sliding glass door across the front of the room opened onto the small porch and the grassy lawn. I had to step out onto the porch to see the house. Inside the room, I was cocooned by gentle light filtering through swaying leaves and long-stemmed flowers. The space felt peaceful, calm, and spiritual. It allowed light as well as privacy.

The rooms of my childhood were different. Back in Allentown, Pennsylvania, I had grown up in a row house in an inner-city neighborhood. We had one bathroom and my mother, father, sister, and even guests had to walk through my bedroom to get to it. When I became a teen, my father took on the project of creating a room just for me in the attic. Two dormer windows allowed light, and he built a desk into each one. He put in a drop ceiling and created cabinets under the sloping walls. I was allowed to decorate it as I wished, which was good because I was in my purple stage. No one ever disturbed me there. That had been my first cocoon.

It was in this now-finished room that my journal became connected with my life with Earle. It was the space that allowed my voice, a voice I poured wholeheartedly into those pages. I had been journaling since 1963, recording life events and thoughts as they happened. But now this book that awaited me and my writing became the vessel for my voice, sacrosanct.

My first entry:

> I am enjoying being in my healing room. It feels good here. It is a comfortable place—my place. It feels cozy. I think it represents me. It is a long time since I felt like I had a nest—since Daddy made over the attic on Meadow Street—just for me. I loved that attic room, and I love this room. The apartments in New York City were not the same—they never felt like home. Living with someone is not the same—all space is shared space. My attic room and my healing room—one and the same—Judy's place.

During this time, I continued to develop my concepts about healing and incorporated them into my teaching. I now understood that there are stages of healing, much as there are stages of grieving. It was important for my students to understand in which stage their patient was, in their process, so they could support the patient in moving on. I had learned other ways to help people heal.

Another workshop, Healing Touch, Level 2B was being offered in Austin that spring.

"Earle, I want to go to this," I said, showing him the brochure.

"That's great," he said. "When you get back, maybe you can practice on me."

I saw and appreciated his smile. I chose to hear his comment as support. But hanging in the background was a niggling thought that it was also a request to be the total center of my attention.

※ ※ ※

Earle's brother rarely called.

"When did it happen?" I heard Earle say into the phone.

Earle came into the living room. He looked sad.

"Mom died today," he said. "We'll need to make travel plans."

Her death was not unexpected. She had been in a nursing home for several years with Alzheimer's disease. I last saw her at the funeral for Earle's father, who had died just before my move to the Rio Grande Valley. We made arrangements for coverage for our classes and flew to Birmingham for his mother's service. After we settled in our hotel that evening, Earle sat down on the bed and pulled up his right pant leg. I was alarmed. His leg was red from ankle to knee, but there we were, away from home.

"Let's just watch it," I said. "Try to keep it elevated as much as you can."

We were on our feet most of the next day, greeting people who came to pay their respects. After the service, family gathered around a light meal, sharing stories and catching up as families do, glad to see each other.

Earle complained about his leg aching.

"Let's take a look," I said.

When I saw it, I called his brother over. We both said the same thing.

"You need to go to the emergency room. Now."

The leg, from knee to ankle was bright, lobster red, skin shiny, with an oozing opening halfway down the shin. The diagnosis was cellulitis, a dangerous situation, especially for a diabetic. His blood sugar still fluctuated even though he had been on medication for six years. He was not consistent in watching his diet. Earle ended up spending a week in a hospital in Birmingham on IV antibiotics. We could not travel back by air until the doctors felt it was safe to do so, and we had to make further arrangements to cover our classes.

When we finally got back home, Earle's leg still had to be monitored to make sure the healing continued. That was my job. Earle could be up and around and was independent, but it had scared him. He made stronger efforts to be careful of his eating pattern. He was still well over two hundred pounds. At five-foot-ten, he was no longer the fit tennis and racquetball player I had married.

Classes ended in May, and Earle was free to enjoy more of his retirement. I was not. I was on a twelve-month contract, and classes continued through the summer. I was absorbed with the responsibilities of preparing our self-study and for the accreditation site visit, scheduled for August.

During the days when I was at work, Earle kept busy with the world of motorcycles. I learned that with motorcycles came accessories, many accessories, and always more and better of everything. The Nomad seemed to attract things like saddlebags, leather fringes, and tassels on the handlebars. Earle's new outfit was made up of the proper helmet, jacket, boots, and pants, all for safety, and rightly so. Then came the unexpected.

I came home one day to find a steel flatbed trailer in our driveway.

"What is that?" I said.

"Well, we need something to haul the motorcycles to events. I had it specially built so that it would accommodate a Goldwing too."

My jaw dropped. He had been talking about Goldwings, especially the large cruiser, giving me a not-so-subtle sales pitch that I worked at tuning out. This was the line: "You should ride a Goldwing to see how it feels. The large cruiser gives such a smooth ride. There's a comfortable seat on the back, and we could have interconnecting radio transmission."

There had been no discussion about purchase. Concern about cost was a knee-jerk reaction for me. These were big-ticket bikes, at least ten thousand dollars. I reminded myself that our finances were now separate, he was receiving retirement income, and they were his purchases, but the unease was there, a tightening of my muscles.

"Did you buy one?" I said.

"Well, not yet," he said. "But I found a used bike that the owner is willing to sell for a couple thousand off."

"Are you asking my permission?" I said.

"Well, I'd like to know what you think," he said.

When he was engrossed in motorcycles, he was joyful. The involvement gave him much to do with his time, and he was not emotionally dependent on me. The two months of recovery from the radiation had been draining on both of us. His depression filled the house. He sat most of the day, watching TV, gloomy. He interacted very little except to complain about something. This was a welcome change.

"Earle," I said. "I remind you that this is out of your pocket—your financial responsibility. Can you handle it?"

"Yes, I can work out a payment plan."

⸳⸳⸳

Looking back, I see this was the beginning point of the new escalation of debt. I also see the continuation of my pattern of not confronting, holding on to a belief that my husband was able to handle his finances, holding on to the fantasy of the husband I wished I had. But I also know the tug I felt at seeing someone who had been weakened by cancer treatment, who was also trying to find his way into retirement.

⸳⸳⸳

I did need relief from the intensity of the accreditation process, and in July, Earle and I took off cross-country, pulling the trailer with the Nomad and Goldwing in place. We were off to the annual Honda Hoot in Asheville, North Carolina. The event drew throngs of motorcycle enthusiasts proudly showing off their bikes. I think Earle rode the Goldwing once the whole time we were there. The rest of the time was about adding more accessories, swapping stories with fun people, kicking tires, and enjoying the beautiful countryside. Earle had given me the gift of a visit to a motorcycle shop to purchase proper boots, padded riding pants and jacket, gloves, rain gear, and a full-face helmet. I was something to behold.

Still, I was glad to get back home. The site visit was only a month away and there was still much to prepare. Earle kept busy with his motorcycle life. All this activity was in contrast to the slow pace of living under intense daily heat indexes of one-hundred-plus.

∽

In the middle of the night, I jolted awake to the sound of moaning. Earle clutched his stomach. It could have been anything, so off to the ER we went. He was admitted to the hospital and the diagnosis was pancreatitis, which is not to be taken lightly. He was treated, and a number of tests were done to try to determine the cause. One such test was an abdominal CAT scan. The next day, Dr. Adams, a nephrologist, came into Earle's room and said the scan showed a funny looking cyst on his right kidney that he felt should be investigated.

"You're here. Let's get a biopsy of that before you leave."

It got done that same day.

Three days later, on our follow-up, the doctor said, "You have renal cell carcinoma. It's a very aggressive cancer, and your right kidney needs to come out right away. We think it's still fully encapsulated, but we need to act fast." We were both stunned. "One other question," he said to Earle. "Do you drink?"

"Only socially," Earle said.

"The reason I ask is that your liver enzymes are not normal."

"Well, that may be because of chemicals I used when I worked as a lab technician in graduate school."

What do I say here? My gut tells me I know the reason, but we've just had a bombshell dropped on us. I didn't speak. Instead, I tucked this information away.

By the end of that same week, Earle's surgeon removed his right kidney. The surgery was major, with a large incision, and Earle was in a great deal of pain afterward. My sister offered to come help for a week, and I welcomed that. She helped with meals, dog care, and extra visits to the hospital when I needed to be at work. The site visit was days away, and the future of our program hung in the balance. My husband had just had major surgery, and we did not yet know what our future held.

The pathology report came back showing that the cancer was indeed still encapsulated and removed successfully along with the kidney. After a week, he was discharged. My sister stayed a day or two longer, then she had to go home to her family. I was now alone with a husband just beginning to recover from a major surgery while our site visitors arrived. It was all about survival at this point. I was too tired to know that I was exhausted.

This recovery was long—August to December. During the first weeks at home, he needed a lot of help, first getting out of bed and then up and out of the recliner. My husband was in a lot of pain. I brought him meals and drinks and took as much time from work as I could. It helped that I did not have a summer teaching assignment. His recovery was slowed by diabetes, the debilitation of major surgery, and poor endurance that lingered from his previous cancer treatment. My husband was sixty-one. We had been married for nineteen years.

Earle was mobile and independent after about four weeks, but then mood swings reappeared, along with anger and frustration at being laid so low. His drinking increased again as well. But he did find times and ways to speak to my heart.

"You are my rock," he said more than once. "I don't know how I could have ever gotten through this without you. I can't tell you how much you mean to me. I love you."

I knew his words were true.

My need for my own healing called me outside and to my sacred space, my healing room. My journal was always waiting, my special book where I could say and think anything. I wrote:

> This has worn me down. I, too, am just now recovering. The constant stress—taking care of—worrying about. It has taken its toll. I am also not what I once was. My joints hurt. I cannot move as quickly. I am not 23 anymore; I am 58.
>
> Where is loving in all this? How am I to be loving in the face of despair, mood swings, anger? How am I to feel sexual, sensual, when I am also living through the fear and the fatigue? It is

hard to switch from support person for a man who is in misery, to lover, eager for his caress.

And now I watch the physical manifestation of his manhood fade. The radiation, the diabetes—both have damaged him too badly. Viagra does not work. He struggles with this, works hard to accept the medical reality. I must be a sensitive, caring lover, and allow myself to be loved as we move through this change in sexuality. Where is the loving? What shape does it take? How are we to love each other?

There were periods of time—the darkest ones—where I was able to hold the light for him. To be there as a positive and loving presence—to hold that energy. I know he felt it. But he is on the mend now, and I don't find the light right now. I don't find it for myself or for him. I struggle with my own changes, my own needs.

We struggled to move forward out of this hard and dark time. Earle moved into the second year of EFM, and I began the program as well. It was something that we could share and do together with like-minded people, and it nourished my spirit.

One sunny morning, just as we had finished breakfast, Earle said, "I'd really like to organize a Goldwing Riders Association Chapter here."

"What a great idea," I said. "You have wonderful organizational skills. It would be totally fun for you."

"OK. I'll get on it." I could feel his energy leap out the door.

For me, the lure was a Healing Touch Level III workshop in New Orleans in mid-fall. The event was a residential week for the purpose of preparing attendees for the formal year of mentorship required for certification. I was sick, running a fever, but I went, along with Sally, Julia—another friend from St. Matthew's—and Jan, a colleague of mine. They were also on the Healing Touch path. As the week went on, I gained a much fuller understanding of the rigor of the year to come.

When I got back, Earle felt well enough to take a short trip with me to Matamoras, Mexico, just across the river from Brownsville. We walked through shops, listened to *Tejano* music, ate Mexican food, and of course had margaritas. It felt good to have a day out.

Two other celebrations arose as 1999 came to a close. The accreditation team from the American Occupational Therapy Association approved our program. We became an independent, freestanding program, and I moved from program coordinator to department chair. The faculties from both the San Antonio program and the University of Texas program came together to celebrate our very hard work. As a group, we walked over the bridge to Reynosa, Mexico, to have a wonderful meal at our favorite place, an Argentinian restaurant called La Mansion. Meals were prepared and cooked to order right at the table. Waiters and chefs were old-school professionals and made the experience most memorable. The restaurant held happy memories for Earle and me as we had hosted our children there on their Christmas visit the year before. Earle totally loved the theatrics of having his Caesar salad prepared fresh at tableside, followed by the flaming orange peel as his dessert was prepared with a flourish.

And then, the other cause for celebration: We learned that in February our first grandchild would arrive; a boy, the proud parents-to-be, Mary and Chris, told us.

A new year renewed hope that the worst was behind us and that 2000 would allow us to move forward in creating what our retirement would be. I had always hoped we would be able to travel widely, perhaps exploring national parks or traveling overseas to places neither of us had ever been. I still had some years to work. I was only fifty-nine. There had been opportunities for Earle and me to do things together, but only in bits and spurts, and always with a timeline. Perhaps we could find space to just be, for however long we wished. Earle was again teaching a few courses during the spring semester and was happy with his continual elaboration on motorcycle accessories and his work with the developing chapter of the Goldwing Riders Association. We were both involved with St. Matthew's and were making good friends.

Tapestry

My workload at the university continued to be heavy as we were now in the process of developing a master's entry-level program, which meant more curriculum development and another accreditation process to come. I still carried a full teaching load. It was hard work, but I loved my students and found the classroom to be a creative place.

The wind here, this close to the Gulf, blows all day long, but at dusk it becomes quiet. The palms that stand to the right of my healing room have their own language of leaves, very different from the sounds of trees in other places I have lived. Hibiscus and bougainvillea flourish in brilliant magentas, yellows, and rich purples, and I love the deep-red hibiscus I planted at a corner of my healing room. The ruby red grapefruit tree and the lemon tree that stand to the left of my healing room fill the yard with the sweet ambrosia of their blossoms in February and March and present us with their fruit in the fall and winter. The Rio Grande Valley is on a migratory pathway, and hummingbirds and red-winged blackbirds, among others, visit us. Permanent residents include kiskadee flycatchers, stunning yellow-bellied birds the size of robins, which chose a tree near my healing room to nest. The neighborhood is also home to several groups of chachalacas, strange-looking brown chicken-like birds that roost in trees and have the unnerving habit of creating horrendous chatter early in the morning and at dusk. And then there are the green anoles, sweet, harmless little lizards that often find their way into our house. On one special day, I saw one sunning on the hibiscus flower by my healing room. Very slowly, I moved my index finger toward it. It looked, then reached out and touched my finger. The touch was as soft and gentle as the feel of a baby's breath, and then it was gone. Suddenly I was connected with spirit, full of awe.

The rhythms of nature, the winds, and the abundant life that surround me become linked with the flow of energy I experience

> when doing Healing Touch, open and selfless. In this natural world I find a beauty that becomes a source of peace for me, a living meditation. The quiet of it, the peace of it, flows into my healing room through open windows on soft breezes, laced with the soft chatter of leaves, birdcalls and the hum of insects, bringing me the nourishment my soul has been longing for all of my adult life—a healing place.

I had begun my year of mentorship in preparation for Healing Touch certification. There was an enormous amount of work involved—case studies, documentation of treatments, readings, and community service. The four of us who were on this journey—myself, Sally, Julia, and Jan—began to meet regularly in my healing room to practice. In the process, we became a support group for each other. I had found my community of women.

We were a rather unlikely group. I was the oldest, fifty-nine now, an academician and occupational therapist. Jan was about five years younger and was the director of the master's in nursing program at the university. She and her husband had lived in the Rio Grande Valley for many years. We worked together in the same building and saw each other often. Her involvement in Healing Touch brought us closer, and we talked about developing an original research study on the effects of Healing Touch on college students.

"I had some experiences when I was young that frightened me at the time," she said as we took our time over a cup of coffee in the university food court. "If I held a personal article of someone, I suddenly was able to see the inside their home, in great detail. I saw personal things about them."

"That's powerful," I said.

"Yes, but it frightened me. I pushed that ability away. I stay away from it. That's why I was reluctant to begin the Healing Touch program when you told me about it. I was afraid that might happen again."

"How did the program affect you?"

"It's such a gentle way of working," she said. "The focus is the flow of energy and being aware of what you are feeling in relationship to that person in that moment in time."

"I find that as well," I said. "It's amazing."

I enjoy Jan's gentle spirit, her kind voice. Her blue eyes and softly waving white hair are lovely. There is a serenity and warmth about her.

I met Sally, ten years younger than me, at St. Matthew's Church. She and her husband have lived in McAllen, the neighboring town, for many years. She is a school nurse in that community, very involved with advocating for her middle school students and supporting their health.

"You know," she said, "those students need so much. They need emotional support, and many of them need to learn daily life skills. I see myself as much more than a nurse in a traditional sense. Their health is about who they are and all that they are involved in."

Sally's energy was vibrant. It enlivened me. She was the sprite of the group, with bright blue eyes and pixie-cut red hair. She was always ready to try new ideas and adventures and read widely about healing in many cultures and traditions.

Julia was the youngest of our group. She was twenty years younger and a school nurse in Edinburg. Julia had a busy life: twin teenage daughters; retired parents who lived across the street from her; an Episcopal priest for a husband, who often substituted at St. Matthew's. Both of them were very involved with the church family.

She and I met once a week for breakfast, with another couple of friends connected with a church group. Julia, tall and slender, arrived with a handful of papers.

"I've brought you all samples of my beginning revision of the Book of Common Prayer," she said. "I think the language has to be modernized big time to incorporate the feminine. I have created generic words throughout."

"Julia. I am really impressed by what you've done," I said. "The changes bring a contemporary perspective, but your language is creative and lyrical as well. Keep at it."

"I play with things like this all the time," she said. "Keeps me awake during boring meetings." Her smile reflected her enjoyment of the process.

Julia and Jan lived on the same street, about a mile from my house. Sally was only fifteen minutes away. Our lives intertwined in many ways, and we knew each other's families, but when we came together with Healing Touch as the focus, we connected with the energies that bound us. Each one of us is a healer. We respected our different skills and sensitivities and learned from each other. I was enhanced by what each person brought. Slowly our bonds became strong in the love and trust we have for each other, and I became aware that I have learned to live "in community," separate from husband and children.

The spring semester was over, and Earle suggested that we take a trip west with the motorcycles. There was a motorcycle meet he wanted to attend in Wichita Falls, Texas, and we worked out a route that would take us there and then on through west Texas into New Mexico with the final destination being White Sands National Monument in Alamogordo. We stayed in KOA campgrounds, which were all very comfortable. It felt good to get away and be out on the open road.

"Let's take a ride to Cloudcroft," Earle said one morning. "We'll take the Goldwing. It'll be fun!"

So, off we went. Cloudcroft is a small village seventeen miles from Alamogordo, straight up. It is a beautiful ride. We came back down on a winding, lovely road through an Apache reservation, then out onto the highway to head back to the campground.

"Guess how fast we're going," came Earle's voice through the intercom in my helmet.

"I have no idea."

"We're going ninety."

I was shocked.

"Please slow down to seventy-five," I said. "That's the speed limit."

He did slow down but went on about how smooth a ride it was. I had to admit, it was.

The last day at the campground, as we were packing up, I savored my memories of White Sands, silent, stunningly beautiful, a place of worship, a still place for my soul. The sputter of a motorcycle brought me out of my reverie. I looked up and watched Earle ride the Goldwing up the ramp of the trailer, and it stalled out. It seemed like slow motion as the bike went down on its side and onto the road. I saw Earle's foot do a one-eighty in the wrong direction as the bike landed on it. I ran over and managed to push it up just enough for him to pull his leg out, and his foot flipped back to its normal position.

"We've got to get the bike loaded," he said. The Nomad was already tied down.

"Earle, your ankle is broken. You can't do it. Stay there. I'll get some help."

He got up anyway and hobbled around to the back of the trailer. Some men at a cabin across the way came when I called for help. They were able to get the heavy Goldwing up the ramp and tied down. Earle was now on the trailer, looking down.

"I think there's something wrong with my ankle," he said. "It feels loose in there."

"Get in. We're going to the hospital," I said, grateful that he was wearing his heavy motorcycle boots. The damage could have been worse.

We were fortunate that the orthopedist on call was a surgeon at the army base in Alamogordo. He was young, bright, and competent.

"He's fractured his right fibula at the base. It will need surgical repair with a plate and screws. We can put him in a light cast, and you can take him home to your own doctor for repair, or we can fix it here today."

"Fix it," I said.

We set off the next morning with a new walker in the back seat. Earle was to be non-weight-bearing for six weeks, meaning he could not touch even part of his foot to the floor. He asked for a Kentucky-blue cast, and it wrapped around from just below his knee to the tip of his toes. The drive was long. Our Buick Le Sabre pulled thousands of pounds of trailer and bike as we navigated winding mountain roads—that is, until we hit

Interstate 10. Sitting next to me was a two-hundred-fifty-pound man, on pain meds, who had never used a walker. We ran out of gas on the Interstate somewhere in the Permian Basin because we did not calculate the effect of all that weight on gas consumption. Fortunately, we were at the top of an exit ramp, and I coasted down. I saw a sign saying there was a gas station two miles away. I got the gallon water container out of the back, threw it at Earle, and said, "Here. Survive. I'm going to walk to the gas station."

I slammed the door, not caring very much at that moment if he survived or not. Fortunately, a very nice couple stopped and gave me a ride to the gas station, then took me back to the car to make sure it started. There are angels everywhere.

Once home in Edinburg, I reverted to caretaker mode. Earle needed a lot of help. In the beginning, he needed guarding when he got up, as he was unsteady with the walker. His walking was limited by his non-weight-bearing status. He did his best, but carrying the bulk of his weight just on his wrists while using the walker gave him wrist and shoulder pain. He needed food and drink brought to him, and he settled into his old pattern of watching old westerns and war movies in between naps. I was grateful for my years of experience as an occupational therapist.

All of this was familiar, but he was supposed to be my partner, not my patient. I did not offer to help with anything that I knew he could do himself, so he took care of his dressing and toileting. I did get a shower chair and wrapped his cast in plastic but then let him do his bathing himself. I was still working full time. It was a long six weeks.

⁓

I went to my healing room, my nest where my journal waited, where peace enfolded me. I wrote:

> In May he broke his ankle. Something happened to me with that. I was angry, and laid so low. The feeling was: Will this never end, this caretaking? How much more must I endure? I was so very depressed—exhausted. Totally depleted. The accident—the three days drive back. Adjusting to a disability,

albeit temporary. The drive back just exhausted me. I must have run out of all reserves. It lasted for weeks and weeks. I have never experienced such a deep, deep pit. There was no love in that place. There was commitment, but no love there. Where was God in that place?

Perhaps it is my own slow decline I fuss at. I cannot do the things I used to when I was 23. How to reconcile a 59 (almost)-year-old body with a youthful mind? I find myself slumping when I walk, must remind myself of my posture. I do last longer than Earle, have more endurance, but then my body has not been irradiated. I am restless with my own decline, my own slowing down. I am not ready for it and it chafes at me.

Earle's fracture healed. He progressed to touch-down weight bearing, then partial weight bearing, then to a boot. Finally, he was independent again. It was a relief for both of us. He had a cancer check-up that showed NED, no evidence of disease.

"What a relief," he said. "It's hard living with a shadow over your head. It's hard to think about moving forward when you don't know if it will be possible."

"I know, I know," I said.

What I thought was, *Do we dare begin to hope again? Hope for normalcy with no disease?* I noticed, though, that there was a perceptible shift in Earle's energy. It was a forward-moving energy, and I was heartened by it. Earle improved so much that we were able to take a day trip to Laguna Atascosa, a wildlife preserve on the bay side of South Padre Island. The variety of water birds fascinated us. We also saw a family of javelina, a hairy, smaller version of something that looked like a pig but was actually a peccary.

Some weeks later, Earle's suggestion to ride the Nomad to Kerrville, Texas, was a welcome adventure. The ride was a long one, and at one point we had to stop on the road and put on our raingear as it started to storm. The road was winding, and we had to go slow, but I never had a moment's doubt about Earle's skill at handling the bike. I felt safe. I trusted him.

⁓

At the beginning of October, a call came at dusk. Another motorcycle accident. It was dark when one of his friends brought him home; another brought his bike.

"I was waiting to pull out onto the highway. My front wheel was on gravel and just slipped out from under me," he said.

We went to the ER. There were no fractures, just a badly bruised forefoot that looked angry and swollen. The doctor was talking about hospitalization, but we went home. I automatically shifted into spouse of sick person, the rhythms now a reflex. He had to keep his leg elevated. We had to wait.

The next morning, he cried. He imagined he saw a red streak from his foot running up the inside of his leg. He was so scared, so vulnerable. I turned on the overhead light and looked and reassured him, as my mother reassured me as a child, that there was nothing there.

Later that day, I was resting on our bed, not sleeping but deep into twilight rest, when I felt I had to get up and try Healing Touch on his foot. I felt as though I was compelled to do that.

"Earle, I want to try some Healing Touch. Is that OK with you?"

"Oh, that would be wonderful."

I sat on a stool next to his foot and wrapped my hands around it, circling the forefoot. I allowed the energy to begin flowing, allowing it to work. I was simply quiet, aware. I began to feel a current flowing between my hands. I began to feel things moving around inside his foot. He said he felt that too. He looked relaxed. I held that position without moving for twenty minutes and then suddenly knew the work was done. My hands cooled, and I let go. We had both fought for his healing.

The next morning, his foot looked much better. The bruising and redness were less, and he said it felt less painful.

"I'm glad it feels better. I'll work on it again this afternoon."

That evening I called my Healing Touch mentor and told her about feeling almost pulled off the bed to work on Earle's foot. I asked her what she thought that was about.

"You were being taught," she said.

That was a powerful learning for me.

In the evening, I went again to my sacred space, my healing room, to my dear journal. I wrote:

> I don't understand. He still talks about the motorcycle, about riding. He is not connecting his slowed reflexes, his diabetes, with his activity. It is as though he doesn't see the danger of this silent disease, perhaps more deadly than the cancer. There is a sensory life for him that is different from mine. Everything for him is big, powerful. He uses huge, sharp knives to cut up small things. I use a paring knife. More and bigger power is his way of seeing life—perhaps that is how he has always lived.

Earle's foot healed well, but by Thanksgiving Eve we were tired. I had to leave the living room, where John Wayne was fighting the Japanese at a volume my ears could not quite tolerate. I retired to my healing room for blessed quiet. I noted that Earle's hearing loss was more pronounced.

We were good now. Earle went after another job and got it. Soft money, grant money, but a position of responsibility with an office. It was wonderful for him. I saw his soul energy absolutely leaping forward. He had decided to embrace life again—he was daring to hope. *This man needs never to retire. He is so energized by people and by meaningful responsibility.*

For me, it was relief. Relief from being the strong one, the responsible one, the caretaker. I had a partner again. It had been so long. I could take care of my own life now.

Earle still struggled. He found it hard, was still so frustrated at being so out of shape. I knew how hard it was to work on changing a lifestyle when one was exhausted, and he was exhausted. This new job, teaching three courses and suddenly back to a forty-hour workweek, no more mornings with old westerns and afternoon naps, would be tough on him. But he was excited about re-entering life as he once knew it.

CHAPTER 8

Turning Point

The mallards, one male and four females, marched off the elevator and onto the red carpet stretching across the lobby of the Peabody Hotel in Memphis. They headed to the large marble fountain in the center of that grand room. The fountain pool was their daytime living space. In the evening, the duck master came and marched them back to the elevator for their trip back to their palatial pen on the roof. People came from far and wide to watch this ritual, and on this day, we were enjoying the show.

It felt good to revisit our past. Earle and I had not been back to Memphis since Mary and Chris were married there five years before, and it brought back many memories for us both. It was the city where we met and where we forged the underpinnings of our life together. It was the place where promises were made.

It was Christmas 2000. Mark and Michelle lived in Memphis, and Mary, Chris, and Katie saw it as a natural place to organize a family get-together to celebrate the holiday and to meet ten-month-old Wyatt,

Mary and Chris's little boy. We all shared memories of that city. We gathered for a wonderful meal in the opulent hotel dining room that feels like old South splendor, lit by the soft light of chandeliers. A lot of wine was consumed at dinner. I was concerned about that, but Earle was well-behaved and social. Katie invited Jen, a classmate friend, to be part of the gathering. Perhaps the presence of a new and neutral person kept Earle mindful of social graces.

Our long road trip to Memphis in Earle's Nissan pickup felt relaxed; it was a good time. It was a chance for us to just be with each other with no distractions. It took a day to get out of Texas to our first stopping point in Texarkana. The next night we spent in our time-share in Lake Hamilton, Arkansas. That break was needed, as we had hit an ice storm that slowed traffic to a crawl across Arkansas. The hours on the road, though, gave us lots of time to talk about whatever came up: our eagerness to see our children; to find out, from them, how they were doing; to talk about the flow of our work and my observations of Earle on his new job. These were the deeper discussions that got lost in the day-to-day scramble of our busy lives.

"I see such joy in you with your new position," I said. "You come home talking about it with excitement. It's wonderful. It feels like a vibrating joy, palpable. Do you feel that?"

A pause settled between us, as Earle seemed caught up in the beauty of ice glistening on the trees in the fields. I followed his gaze and was drawn into the wonder of each individual leaf, blade of grass, and cornstalk encased in a shimmering cover. A place of fragile peace. He shifted his hands on the steering wheel, resettled his weight, then said, "I've been in such a period of loss for such a long time, with the move, the cancers, and the accidents. What feels so good now is that I see myself as having value again."

"I'm truly glad for you," I said.

I meant it.

After Memphis, moods shifted. The last two days of our trip home, Earle slipped back into a negative place. The pattern was almost predictable now. Times of blessings and joy, such as our visit with our children, followed by a downward slide into dark moods. I know he didn't feel well. He had caught the cold I had the week before and was congested and probably feverish.

His negativism became so powerful that I felt as though darkness was invading me and pushing all my positive feelings away. His body became tighter, more rigid. Eye contact disappeared. He cursed at the slightest thing. He interpreted every event to be something someone wanted to do to him. The day before was nice. We went into a motorcycle shop that he wanted to see. We stopped at a bookstore he wanted to go to. But as we got within about fifty miles of home, his mood darkened again.

"I've got to go to the bathroom," he said.

I pulled into the next gas station we came to. He got out, moving his bulk slowly, but soon came back to the car.

"The toilet is out of order," he muttered. "You can tell we're back in the Valley," he said with disgust.

We went on to the next gas station, which was fine, and then finally arrived home. He was cranky all evening, irritated because food that he thought was going to be there was not, that the garbage cans were still on the curb, and that plastic bags had blown into the driveway. Later we were sitting in the living room, winding down. I was reading *LIFE* magazine, and he was watching a sports event on TV. Suddenly, he yelled at me.

"I know what's coming!" he said. "You don't like that kind of show. I'll just go into the other room."

It was out of the blue. I was reading the magazine, not paying any attention to the TV. I felt angry, but I knew better than to talk with him at that point. He would not have been able to hear anyway. What I wanted to do in that moment was to yell back at him how attacked I felt. How unpleasant and unfair he was. How he made an assumption and didn't check it out, as we had agreed to do years before. But I waited.

The next morning, I was able to tell him how I felt. He got huffy but apologized. I took time to retreat to my place of peace, my healing room, my journal. I wrote:

Turning Point

It's odd. I ended up feeling like I know he loves me and cares about me and needs me, but it's almost like sometimes he doesn't like me very much.

What he wants from me is to be fussed over and rubbed and massaged and petted and pampered and paid much attention. I just didn't have it in me last night. I didn't feel well either—was tired—needed to unwind. I think if I had petted and pampered him his mood would have been different. But I felt like I was there for him for the whole trip—and just didn't have anything left.

I find myself an observer of this man as he travels his life path. He ate too much on this trip. He must have stopped checking his blood sugars some weeks before—am not sure how long. It must have been out of control because on our drive to Memphis he had to stop every half-hour, urgently, to pee and was very thirsty. Both signs of blood sugar that was too high. The same with our trip back.

I do not understand how he can be blind to what he needs to do to help himself. He is a man of moods and passions and seems unable to control or moderate them. I am concerned for his health. I feel like I am watching someone self-destruct, but there is nothing I can do. If I try to provide the structure, then it always ends up being interpreted as "getting on his case." It is not my life path; it is his. I have let go and allow him his journey.

But I feel compassion as well. On the trip, I saw him struggle with his bowel and bladder needs. He is, in effect, controlled by his body not working well. How miserable that must be for a proud man. He struggles to get his bulk in and out of the car. His movements are stiff, his muscles tight. His body is thick and inflexible. He must feel physically not good all the time. I am sure some of that reflects in his mood. He is trapped and can find no way out for himself. I feel sorrow for him. I pray for him.

The beginning of the academic year of 2001 saw improvement in Earle's mood. He was enjoying his new grant-funded project and was engaged with his students.

We were able to find time to play again. When I went to a national professional conference in Orlando, Earle came along.

"Let's take a day to go to Disney World," I said. "I've never been."

"Would love to," he said.

We had fun—walked a lot, saw a lot, but by the end of the day, he was clearly very tired. He did not talk as much, his walking slowed, and his face was empty of expression.

"Time to go back to our hotel and get a good sleep before our cruise," I said.

That surprise had been dropped in my lap a few weeks before the conference. Earle came home one evening, looking like a cat that had just fallen into a bowl of catnip.

"I won a trip," he said, beaming. "And it won't cost us a thing. We just have to go hear a time-share presentation."

He explained how he had seen the raffle at a home show and dropped his name in the box. He was chosen.

"The timing is perfect," he said. "We can just add those few days to our trip to Orlando."

It took some negotiation, but we were able to do that. Neither one of us had ever been on a cruise. I totally enjoyed the experience. I felt pampered. Earle enjoyed the availability of unending food and drink. On the final night, after dinner, the crew put on a show for the guests. Earle got up from the table.

"I need to go to the bathroom," he said, and left.

He did not return for a long time and I was wondering where he had gotten to. Finally, he came back and settled into his chair.

"I didn't make it," he said.

He had been gone so long because he had to go back to the room to change clothes. I then noticed that he was now wearing jeans when before he had been wearing khakis. I could feel his embarrassment.

Turning Point

☙ ☙ ☙

The next months kept us busy. In February, we went to the Kick-Off for Chapter Five of the Goldwing Riders Association on South Padre Island. The event lasted the weekend, with contests, prizes of all kinds for motorcycles, and the camaraderie that develops among people who have worked hard for a common goal. Earle had spearheaded the chapter development, and I was very proud of him and his success.

We were both re-engaged with Education for Ministry, and I had joined a new group at church called Community of Hope. It was a structured program that guided participants into exploring pastoral care in the real world.

In addition, Earle had discovered a camera club. Photography became his new passion. Cameras began to appear around the house as well as all kinds of accessories: camera cases, tripods, more and better lenses, and he enrolled in online camera courses. My concern grew, again, about how much all of these things cost. I tried to remind myself that none of the costs were coming out of my pocket. But I couldn't quite shake the worry.

We had planned for some time to attend Katie's May graduation from her nursing program in Portland, Maine. A week before we were to leave Earle started to complain that he couldn't pee—he just couldn't pee. By that night, he was in such pain that we went to the ER. The cause was a urinary-tract bleed that clotted. The clots blocked the urine flow. Earle's bladder had to be irrigated for a half-hour before the saline flowed clear. The doctor told us the bleed was secondary to his prostate being softened by radiation. It was just something to be watched. He told us if it happened again to increase fluids and just watch. We went ahead to the graduation. I wanted so badly to go and trusted the doctor's opinion that this could be managed if it happened again. It felt so good to celebrate Katie's success. The whole family was there. Earle did have another bleed, but it stopped on its own. Just another side effect from a treatment that was given four years before.

I returned home, eager for my healing room. The spring evening air felt soft and gentle around me. Scents and sounds, so familiar now, fed my spirit. I became still as I found my center, my inner quiet place, and began to feel the peace. I wrote:

> There is interruption in my life with these events, but somehow not so draining this time. I find myself moving toward more and more objectivity about this man I live with, my husband, my friend, my high-maintenance man.
>
> So, where does Judy fit into this picture? How do I deal with this? I find myself reacting in a very objective way. If I indeed am seeing what I think I am seeing, there are huge implications and challenges for the future, and I must take care of and protect myself. But I also find myself loving this man more than ever, with caring and compassion. He has endured much and has carried most of it with courage and honor and dignity. I respect and admire him for his struggle to learn and grow. I see him learning from EFM. He tries, he works at it. I love his vitality, his energy when he is feeling well. As much as he is negative with me, he also adores me and sees what I give him. He can be great fun. He lives his life to the fullest. I am committed to this man. I think back to that long-ago conversation in a car in Memphis. I wonder if I have already begun to help him die.

I was learning how to deal with the mood swings. I tried to let them roll off, and most of the time I succeeded. Things had been very slow at work for him—in his mind he saw nothing to do and could not find structure. He slept a lot and seemed tired. He truly did not have reserves of endurance. When he perceived he had "nothing to do" at work, he got to feeling bad about himself and dumped on me.

"You never want to go to the motorcycle meetings with me," he said one evening. "I know you think it's no fun going anywhere with a fat old man."

There was a time when I would have argued, telling him that was not the case and I didn't feel that way at all. I would get pulled into his pattern of baiting me only to argue without an endpoint. I knew this now and no longer accepted it as my issue. I could walk away.

◎ ◎ ◎

The occasional memory and confusion issues I noticed back in 1998, when Earle first moved to Texas, appeared again on the trip back from Maine. We landed in Houston to connect with our flight to McAllen and identified our gate on the monitors. Signs were clear and well-marked. Suddenly, it was gone for him. He couldn't remember what we had talked through less than three minutes before, and there was confusion with it. I knew he was fatigued—our schedules were off, but the episode of confusion lasted about five minutes.

Once home, we met some friends for lunch, and it happened again. Earle was chatting on and on, telling stories about our trip and talking about the ages of the children and about Michelle specifically. We were talking about how old Michelle is now and how old Mary is.

Suddenly, he looked at me and said, "Then why did Michelle and Mary graduate together?" His face was full of puzzlement.

"They didn't," I said.

After a pause, he said, "Oh, yes, they played soccer together." He looked around the table at the others. "It all runs together," he said with a little laugh.

To others, this hiccup in memory might seem commonplace, but I saw the difference from the sharp, incisive thinking of the man I married. It wasn't just the forgetting. I forgot too. What concerned me was the confusion that seemed to go with it, albeit fleeting. It caused me to think back and reflect. My gut feeling was that he had been having trouble handling his job for some time before I left Lexington. I did not think there was any way now that he could handle a full-time, high-pressure administrative job. I wondered if his storytelling, which he enjoyed, had allowed him to cover slips in memory. He had always enhanced his telling of events. When I corrected him, he got angry.

I wondered: *Was I seeing a precursor to Alzheimer's?* I knew there were other possible explanations. Damage to small vessels from years of not-very-well-controlled diabetes. Two cancers. Depression. My many years as an occupational therapist, treating thousands of clients in all stages of illness, reinforced the thought that there was some neurological process going on.

A large portrait of Dr. Lana Villalobos was mounted on the wall of her waiting room, looking down over everyone. Earle and I had been patients of hers for a while, so when she walked into the exam room to greet him wearing her stiletto heels, leopard-spotted skirt, and a draped top that revealed just a hint of cleavage, I was not that startled. I smiled to myself as I watched the dance between my husband and his doctor.

Ah, a match. She is drama with total awareness but also has excellent professional skills. He is drama, also with excellent professional skills. They connect. He takes in her clothing, appraising the effect, enjoying it. As she moves around him during her examination his eyes drop, enjoying. She is fully aware of this. I must not chuckle out loud. He totally listens to her.

"Earle, you are too fat," she said. "Your blood sugar is out of control. I'm putting you on a 1,500 calorie ADA diet. I want to see you back here in three months, and I want results."

She got right in his face, as I had learned was her style. He lost nineteen pounds in the first month, and I knew I had found an ally in Dr. V.

Word came that the grant Earle had been working under for the past year was not funded again. Then the dean seemed to be waffling on an assistant dean position that she was considering for him. It was July 2001, and he slid into depression. This one was much deeper than usual.

"I feel hopeless. Another loss," he said. "You'd be better off with me gone."

He was sitting in his recliner, head hanging low, shoulders slumped, looking almost tearful.

"You've got an appointment with Dr. V coming soon," I said. "You have to talk to her about how you're feeling. It's time to ask her about antidepressant medication."

I was firm and direct. He said he would. Later I called her and told her that I had asked him to talk with her about his depression. She promised she'd get to it if he didn't bring it up. She also promised confidentiality. Then I stepped back. I did not prompt him before his visit. He did bring it up, and she did put him on an antidepressant.

A month later, I could not believe the difference. The heavy mood was gone. He laughed in a way that was truly different. It bubbled up, flowed. I could share in that; I could join him. His energy improved. There was a lightness about him. This was a new man. I thought he must have been depressed for the past twenty years and probably beyond. Perhaps we could now have a normal life.

> Normal. What was that? I would welcome that. I felt sorrow for our 20 years of a roller coaster life. I felt sorrow for its impact on me, and I think that has been enormous. It has been such a drain on my life energies. What a toll. Has it dampened me? I thought so. I felt grief about this. So many years with all my energies going to coping with this. I did not feel anger—it was an illness. But I felt such sorrow. I wanted him well for the rest of my life.

The dean finally made a decision to appoint Earle as an assistant dean, on an emergency hire line item. She needed help, and he was a fine administrator. He functioned well in this familiar role and was well-liked and appreciated for his skill. The year rolled on smoothly. We were able to find time to travel north in the summer to Binghamton, New York, to visit Mary, Chris, and little Wyatt, and then on to Pennsylvania to visit my sister and her family. We continued with our church activities, and Earle pursued his photography and motorcycle passions. A summer highpoint was a dolphin-watching boat trip into the Gulf of Mexico that we both totally enjoyed. At the end of the year, he organized a sixtieth birthday party for me. I was so appreciative that he thought to do that.

Then, upheaval.

"My position has not been renewed," he said as he came in the door from work. "I know it's the provost. He has never liked me. He has something against me. He wants me out." Earle was angry now.

"Earle. I know it's a blow, but I'm convinced it was a purely financial decision," I said. "I have been on the administrative end of my program for four years now. We work for the same university. I know how the provost thinks. It is all about money to him, and the university is under financial stress right now."

"I don't believe that. He has had something against me for a long time."

I saw that, for now, the thought was fixed. Earle had voiced this before about others. Mostly people in positions of authority.

He took a week to clear out his office, refigured finances, and filed for Social Security. He would teach three courses as an adjunct.

"I feel such a loss again. I really enjoyed the assistant dean position and now it's gone. This time I'm really ready for retirement. After all, I started this early retirement process four years ago when I was fifty-nine."

A week after classes started, a student filed a written complaint about Earle's behavior in the classroom.

"What caused the complaint?" I said.

"She said the language I used was sexist," he said.

I felt my jaw drop.

"So, I took the letter to class the next day and read it to everyone," he said.

"I can't believe you did that." I was shocked at his lack of judgment and also afraid there might be an institutional consequence.

The result was that all the students then filed a harassment charge and threatened to sue. Earle was called into the dean's office and got abundant feedback from the Equal Employment Opportunity Commission officer, the dean, and another faculty member. What he did was not terrible but showed very poor judgment with no awareness of consequences. This was the man who had once been the EEOC officer for the University of Tennessee-Memphis.

A week later, we were in church for Rally Day. The priest asked Earle to take forty-five seconds to briefly describe a program he was mentoring. His instruction was "we just want people to know we are doing things." At least six others were scheduled to speak after him. When Earle got up, he said, "I can't do this in forty-five seconds." He was able to stay on topic for only a few seconds, then began to ramble, talking about other events—how he liked to slice meat at the barbecue, how he had attended a weekend workshop and how much it meant to him. His speech was rambling and tangential. He went on for probably three minutes before finally coming back to topic for a second or two. I caught his eye and gave him the cutthroat sign, and he said, "Oh, I see my wife says it's time to stop." Then he sat down, with no apparent awareness of what he had just done. I was very alarmed.

He slept almost the whole weekend after that. He talked very little. He tried to work on his computer a bit and watched some football. I had suspected sleep apnea for a long time, and it had grown worse over the past six months. I was concerned and asked him to talk to Dr. V about it.

I noticed his inertia. He was apathetic and passive with times of confusion. I wanted so badly for him to be helped so I could be helped. I wanted to know what I was up against so I could develop a shape for my life.

So, I talked with Dr. V myself and asked for a total medical evaluation. She agreed.

I was drawn to my place of peace, my healing room. My place of solace. I wrote, trying to sort things out:

> I am so sad and tired tonight. I feel the reality of Earle slipping away. Perhaps the sleep apnea treatment will help—when he finally agrees to go get it done—but there has been another weekend of seeing him slide. We went to South Padre Island, just 85 miles away, for a professional conference I was involved in. He loves the Gulf so I hoped he would feel better there. He was very passive. He lets me drive all of the time now. When we got there,

it was late. He slept off and on all day the next day—and did not leave the hotel. So very unusual. The last morning, he could not figure out how to plug in the microwave. Just stood there and said, "It won't work." He could not problem-solve finding the outlet and plugging it in. It is so sad. I have been pushing him like crazy to see the doctor, thinking this can be fixed, but I am so afraid that it is too late. The decline has been very fast—this last six months. And I think it is just too late. But then some days he seems pretty good. He has been sweating a lot. Just sits there and sweats—diaphoretic. He forgets to take his meds sometimes. I just want to cry. I am so very sad. It is a deep, deep sadness. I love him. It wasn't supposed to be like this. It just wasn't supposed to be like this. We were supposed to do things together and enjoy life. I cry inside.

As 2003 began, I couldn't escape what I was seeing. Earle drank a lot, episodically. He spent a lot, episodically; he ate a lot, almost all of the time. His weight increased to three hundred and ten pounds with blood sugar out of control. He could not stay awake.

Trying to climb out of denial is like trying to climb out of a pool of molasses. The pool is dark and sticky. The molasses gets all over you and sticks your parts together. It is not comfortable, but it has a smell that reminds you of the comfort of syrup on pancakes—a pleasant, almost bitter, burnt-sugar taste that leaves you wanting just a bit more. It is about comfort and all that has fed you. It is about learned patterns that were not of your making but stick your parts together nonetheless.

I knew that Al-Anon existed. That knowledge came through my work as a health-care professional. But Al-Anon was for other people. My first knowledge of it as it related to me was when I called an acquaintance who was an accountant for a bank. I wanted advice on how to deal with a husband who was spending us into enormous debt. She offered suggestions on how to protect myself financially, but as I talked in more detail about his issues around drinking, she firmly but with caring suggested I seek out Al-Anon. Her suggestion made me very anxious. Al-Anon! For me? That would mean there was something wrong with our marriage! That would mean that perhaps I had some responsibility in what was wrong! I was shaken. It pushed me to the edge of that sticky pool, but I could only put out one finger to tap around and explore what was there.

It took me a year to take action. I could not ignore my husband's addictive behavior. It was in my face. But confronting it was hard for me to do because in my growing up, I learned that avoiding confrontation was what one did. One evening, after dinner, we were sitting in the living room. Earle had his water glass full of wine in one hand and the remote control for the TV in the other. Before he could turn on the TV, I brought up AA and suggested in a direct and honest way that he go. He looked at me and asked if I thought he was an alcoholic. I said, "Yes." He paused for a minute, then turned on the TV. He never went. I came to understand that I had to take action for myself. I did not want to drown in the sticky pool.

I looked up Al-Anon in the phone book, called the number, and got a recording of meeting times and places. I found the nearest one that would fit my work schedule. The meetings were held once a week in an old red brick Methodist church during lunch. The day of the first meeting came. I told my husband where I was going. He did not say anything, and I could not read his expression. Some fear, perhaps. And out the door I went.

The drive to the church was not long, perhaps fifteen minutes. Entering the church, I steeled myself. *This has to be done*, I told myself. I felt the terror in the tightness of my body and the clenching of my gut at entering new territory. I walked through the door, down a long hallway, and into a rather drab meeting room. Tables were set up in a large square with perhaps a dozen women already seated. I noticed books on the table. I found that I was trembling, my hands shaking. I could not speak except to say hello. I had come face-to-face with almost a lifetime pattern of denial, and the wall was suddenly crumbling down. I was powerless to stop it. I felt naked, laid bare.

I walked over to the table, pulled out a metal folding chair, and sat down. I was without words. My face felt frozen, locked down. I had trouble making eye contact, trying to take in the others present with quick, half-hidden glances. Someone put a sign-up sheet in front of me and said to just write my first name. The woman next to me reached over and touched my arm. She said gently, "You are not the only one who loves an alcoholic." Those quiet words shattered the dam, and the tears streamed down my face in sheets, a blessed release.

The Serenity Prayer soothed my heart, and the Lord's Prayer with everyone holding hands at the end completed the feeling of connection. I listened to the readings and the discussion and was able to see that I was not alone.

How simple. I had made a decision to go to a meeting. In doing so, I stepped out of the pool of molasses and began to find the tools that would help me stay on firm ground. I moved into enormous learning about who I was, within a safe community of support. It was a step toward health and strength, which would lead me to my truth.

☙ ☙ ☙

As part of Earle's full medical evaluation, a small ischemic area, an area showing inadequate blood supply, was found on his heart. A cardiac catheterization was done to check this out and showed no blockage. I was relieved, and so was Earle.

Slowly, the sleep apnea was being addressed. I had grown used to sleeping lightly, giving him a push when I heard him stop breathing. This happened numerous times each night. We were both eager for the CPAP machine that would allow him to breathe normally while sleeping. Perhaps then he would have more energy. Our reality was that he slept more than he was awake, and I was essentially alone. I struggled with those feelings. I still felt anger that he didn't help with household tasks. But I also saw that he was not well and had nothing to give me now. When I tried to talk with him about my needs, he went into a guilt sort of thing. I was tired of that.

I chose not to talk with him about some things now. It was also easier to just let him sleep—I had learned that I must let go. As someone in Al-Anon said, "Honey, give him to God and don't take him back."

∽

It was a springtime evening. My healing room had become a place for quiet reflection without judgment. I went there frequently now, sometimes to see Healing Touch clients, sometimes to connect with my spirit, my soul, the deepest part of me. And my journal was always there, waiting:

> Al-Anon helped me understand the decade of hell in our life together, the years from the mid-80s to mid-90s. Drinking, arguments, outbursts, mood swings, emotional manipulation. I am now in a period of new growth. And so, this writing must switch to writing about my growing and not Earle's holding me back. I am holding me back. He is an ill person in my life, whom I will love and support but cannot rescue.
>
> Earle's dependence on me sucks me down. Sometimes I can detach and love him, but tonight I feel so depleted by this 64-year-old two-year-old I live with. I am angry with all of this—angry at him, at myself, for being in this place. It's hard to get out of it right now. I think the root of it is not taking care of myself. I decided to do that tonight.

"I am not going to EFM," I said.

For a flash he looked angry with me. There was a lot I did not want to be doing right then. I did not want to go to EFM, to church, to tai chi, to work. I guess I just didn't want to do anything at all except what I wanted to do.

That night, I thought about letting go of being chair of the program. I wanted to complete that responsibility, but I needed to listen to my intuition to understand when it was finished. I could still be faculty.

Another thought entered my mind: Earle's diarrhea and urinary urgency tied us down, severely limiting what we could do together. It seemed worse lately—perhaps because of the increased diuretic. This was something he could not control. For me, it took patience and tolerance to live with. I thought I had done well with that. Some days he did well, but he had been very tired again the past two days. All of this was tiring for me.

So, what was I doing about it? I needed to read my Al-Anon materials. I needed to paint. I needed to not run away from my feelings. Moving into my marriage with Earle, with all the attendant complexity of blending families, had not allowed time to process feelings about my former marriage. I was not ready to address what I wanted to do with Judy at that point in my life. I could escape into "us"—the illusion of partnership with Earle. The illusion of safety and stability. I did not work on myself then. But I was now and had been since 1996, when I moved to Texas—slowly, slowly, and now with help and support from Al-Anon. Now was indeed the time.

※ ※ ※

In looking at me, I had to face what I saw around myself. A mountain of goods had accumulated in Earle's office—a new computer, printer, camera gear of all sorts, motorcycle paraphernalia, office supplies, and more. I might as well have been looking at a room full of dollar bills. I decided it was time to deal with this. It was 2003, five years since all of our debts had been paid off. One afternoon, when he was out shopping, I went into his office and started going through his bills. I recorded what I found and could no longer avoid.

When he returned, I asked him to sit down with me at the dining table. "Earle, I need to talk with you about something."

"Oh, OK. Let me put this in my office." He was carrying a bag from Staples. "What do you want to talk about?"

"I went through your bills this afternoon and added up the balances. I found thirteen credit cards, with a cumulative balance due of $65,000."

He just looked at me.

"I will not live this way anymore. You have to take care of this. Fix it." Suddenly, tears burned my eyes, but my voice was strong. "I will not live with debt anymore. I have done that for almost all the years we've been married, and I cannot and will not do it any longer." I never felt stronger.

"I didn't know you felt that way," he said. I could not tell if he was shaken by the amount, but I could see that he was shaken by what I was saying. Tears welled up in his eyes too.

"I don't know what to do," he said. "Can you forgive me?

"I think you have an addiction. Expenditures are about choices," I said. "This is a chance for a new beginning. I'll help you find a debt reduction company to help you work out what has to happen, but you have to deal with them. Think about this. What is your responsibility to our lives? What is your responsibility to yourself?"

He agreed to my plan.

❦

The Healing Touch group met later that week. I could not wait to find shelter and support among my friends. I shared it all: the shock and the anger and the frustration. They understood that I did not need advice. I needed simply to be heard. That was a blessing.

❦

It was mid-May 2003, and I was having trouble sleeping. A crisis cluster, as my daughter Mary puts it. Earle's gastric bypass surgery had gone awry. He had decided months ago that the solution for his weight problems was a gastric bypass. We found a hospital in Harlingen, Texas, that was performing these surgeries, and he entered the program. Preliminary interviews, studies, and tests were very thorough, and he was judged fit for the procedure. But the surgeon came to his room after Earle returned from surgery and told us he did not do the bypass.

"I found significant cirrhosis of the liver, an enlarged spleen, and evidence of portal hypertension," he said. "The surgical procedure involved was beyond the capacity of Earle's body to handle. I even called a liver specialist to the OR to consult on this. I'm sorry. 'Do no harm' is my first consideration."

❦

That night, when I returned home from the hospital, I embraced my journal again.

Tapestry

Earle's long-term abuse of his body has caught up to him, and now we both pay. I am angry tonight—not at this illness, but at our financial situation. But I guess that is part of the illness. I hate the illness of alcoholism and what it has done to our lives—my life. Stocks continue to drop. Earle's retirement income has fallen again. It would not be so bad if he had not charged up the amount that he did. We carry that load. I feel self-anger about not seeing that, about being in denial for so long. I was part of the illness to be sure. Perhaps the essence is, can I love myself, accepting all of these feelings?

I am tired tonight. I am having trouble letting go. Mary's Mother's Day card brought tears to my eyes. It was such a statement of love from her. It was a gift. And it was also a gift in that I can receive that love and understand that I am deserving of it.

I must continue to be careful in taking care of myself in my fatigue—to pay attention to that which I must do for myself. I have made some gains in this.

So, I find myself, at this late hour, wondering what is in this lesson for me in my lifetime. I see myself in a life of struggle, but a life also of incredible beauty. I understand that my life of struggle is no different than millions of others on this planet. I feel as one with all those others with grief to bear, battles to fight, personal challenges to overcome. It is a Herculean task we all take on—our lessons in this lifetime. Heroic is the word. We live lives of heroism. There is no utopia. I finally understand that. I think that is one of my lessons. Life is like the ocean—swirling currents, calm spots, storms, incredible beauty, full of life-forms, the stuff from which we are made in our cells, our mother, our source. We are tossed and supported at the same time. Yes, I think that is one of my lessons—to see my commonality with humanity for what it is, not what I fantasize it to be.

Another lesson: I can give up being a martyr. And when I let that go, it leaves a space for other things to come in, such as appreciation and gratitude for all the love that is genuinely in this world for me. So now my issue is to continue to take care of myself and to live in the present moment doing only what it is reasonable to do this day.

The day after the Fourth of July was a shitty day, and I didn't know why. I'd had fun cooking—trying out some new recipes. Earle had been patient with my experimenting. But the house was a wreck. I tried to wait for him to do things, but he would fall asleep or get lost in the TV. I think what got to me was that there was always so much clutter. He had so much stuff and he couldn't get rid of it. Or he would forget he had it because he had so much stuff. And the TV was *always* on; I could scream sometimes with the never-ending sound. So, I fled to my healing room—my escape.

What am I to learn from this? What am I to learn from him? Certainly patience. I have indeed learned about the impact of my expectations, for all those in my life, but also for myself.

One morning, we went for a walk. Earle was recovering nicely from the failed bariatric abdominal surgery, or so I thought. We walked for twenty minutes. He barely made it. He said his back hurt. He was walking in a forward-flexed position much of the time, and his back had kinked up, so he had to stop. I was afraid he was going to fall.

Earle still had to dress up in the appropriate clothing; he always felt a need to "look the part." It was eighty degrees or more outside, with a heat index higher than that, and he had on shorts, two pairs of socks, and hiking boots. When we got home, he sat down in the chair and fell asleep. This confirmed my thoughts about a vacation that we had planned—a three-week driving tour of the southwest. My expectations were that I would do ninety-five percent of the driving and that we would do very little in terms of hiking, even on smooth walking trails. If we did have a day on which we hiked, I expected that the next day he would need to sleep most of the day. Still, the vacation would be enjoyable because the scenery would be new to us. I decided we had to do this trip, as we might not have another chance.

☙

We did go on the vacation, and we had the most wonderful time we have ever had. It was amazing; transformative. Earle was able to do just about half the driving. He tried very hard to keep up and did well. He let me know his physical limits at times, and we accommodated each other. We experienced joy in new discoveries every day. Free from responsibilities and worries, I was able to have fun. And he enjoyed my doing that. We had a ball. Sometimes I found myself reciting the first line of the Serenity Prayer. "God grant me the serenity to accept the things I cannot change . . ." It was helpful. I was able to drop expectations of Earle, and myself as well, and so we were able to truly enjoy each other.

I felt as though we were falling in love all over again, but in a truer way. I felt such love for this man. He was genuinely wonderful in many ways. He was patient and loving and supportive with me. He slipped a few times with drinking, but I was able to structure that, and limit it, in a way that was not blaming. I linked it to the amount of money we had to spend per day.

And so, it was the trip of a lifetime. We drove west, across Navajo and Hopi lands, then north into Utah to Bryce Canyon. Turning south, we moved through Nevada and took in the Hoover Dam, then saw Las Vegas from the highway. Our journey led us back into Arizona, through Kingman, for a stop at a time-share in Sedona for a few days. We lingered in that stunning beauty before heading back to Texas, through the Painted Desert and Petrified Forest. I was so very grateful.

☙ ☙ ☙

I was not blind. Earle remained unwell. He still tired easily, slept a lot, and needed guidance at times. But when we got back, he was able to teach two courses, and I was grateful for that. He had good intentions. He tried. For the most part, I was able to deal with spills and messes. Something had transformed me, and I must assume it was God. I could certainly not do this by my own will. I had tried that for too many years.

CHAPTER 9

New Directions

I liked knowing that when the four of us gathered in Gram's living room for our group, I would be folded in by the warmth and uniqueness each woman brought. Sally would surprise and cheer. Julia would find the beanbag, and Jan often brought a treat. This evening was no different, with Julia already deep in the dark-blue beanbag so as to accommodate her lanky, long-legged frame. Then Jan came with a platter of oatmeal cookies. "Fresh-baked," she said. "I'll put the kettle on for tea," she added and busied herself in the utility kitchen. Sure enough, Sally's cheery voice, "I brought fairy dust," announced her arrival. In she came with a tiny bottle of glitter for each of us. "You can sprinkle some on yourself whenever you need it." She handed each of us a small container and settled herself cross-legged in a corner of the big leather couch.

We'd grown close over the years. We used to call ourselves the Healing Touch group, but now we are just "the group." Our bond is one of trust, caring, and sharing. We first came together to practice techniques back in 2000, when we had all completed the required workshops to put us into our mentorship year for certification. In those days, we met in my healing room, sitting on big pillows on the floor, breezes blowing through the curtains in the place that was my sacred space. We set candles around us on the floor and on my desk and bookshelf as well, which helped focus our attention on our goals. We practiced, talked about our work on case studies and about the requirements for certification. We shared experiences we had while doing the energy work and met every four to six weeks. Each of us brought our own unique selves to that group, and each of us was directly involved in health care. We understood each other's professional language and workplace challenges. Over time, we got to know each other's personal challenges as well.

About a year ago, Julia's grandmother died. She was a character, much loved by her family. She lived in a tiny house, the *casita,* set off by itself behind the house Julia and her husband and daughters lived in. It had been perfect for her. Gram, as she was called, had her own space but was close enough to be part of the family. After she died, the house sat unoccupied.

One day when we were meeting, Julia brought an idea to us.

"You're all welcome to meet at Gram's casita," she said. "It's not being used and might give us a bit more space. I think she would like if we met there."

There was some discussion, mainly around not wanting me to feel like they didn't like the healing room. But I agreed totally that the casita would be more comfortable. It was small, with a bedroom, living room, small bathroom, and kitchenette. The color scheme was simple: brown. It was decorated with old but serviceable brown furniture, brown paneled walls, and some neutral throw rugs. It felt homey. The lamps provided enough light to be serviceable, and Gram's knick-knacks and pictures still decorated the rooms. It became our meeting place, and I had the community of women for which I had longed.

By 2003, we knew pretty much everything about each other. The Healing Touch focus had shifted over time to include unconditional support for everyone as we navigated the problems unique to each of us in our lives. These women knew about my life with Earle and had been there for every tough time that came along.

When we were settled, we started what had become our routine. We went around the room and everyone gave a summary of what had gone on since the last time we met. Julia had challenges with her teenage daughters. Sally's husband was stuck in a pattern of golf and football, and she struggled with that relationship. Jan was dealing with work and stepdaughter issues. I brought them up to date with Earle's progress on his debt.

"I think everything is ready for finalizing his contract with the debt consolidation company," I said. "The hardest thing for him so far is that the contract required that he destroy all of his credit cards. That was incredibly hard for him to do."

"How did you handle that?" Sally said. "That's got to have been so hard."

"It was. I stood next to him and handed him the scissors. I stood there until he was done."

"What did he say about it?" Julia said.

"He didn't say anything, but it was the slowest I've ever seen him move. I think he's depressed," I said. "I'm sure he had fantasies about how much money he had and was truly enjoying spending it in his mind. That's now at an end."

"You know, Judy," Jan began. "When I think back, having known you now since you started at the university, and knowing your story, I think Earle's cascade of illnesses began when you moved here and the two of you were apart for those two years."

"I've had that thought, too, Jan," I said. "It seems more than coincidence. I think there might be many reasons: the stress of living alone for two years, the long years of his abuse of alcohol and food, moving to Lexington where he never felt support after working for seventeen years in a different university system where he did feel supported and appreciated. That was a huge change. But he lived his life making his own decisions, his own choices about behavior, as we all do. All I know is that we were drawn to each other to walk side by side, living each day as it came."

I was quiet, allowing space, then I said, "I can't tell you how much your friendship and support has meant to me over these past years. There were times I just had to cry my heart out. Knowing that I was with people who understood meant the world to me."

"We all have times like that in our lives," Sally said. "What we are together is a safe place."

Everyone nodded in agreement. We went on with other discussion, then identified the time for our next meeting. On the way out the door, Julia said, "Please take all the papaya that you want. I just picked them from our tree this afternoon."

☙ ☙ ☙

Earle and I celebrated his sixty-fifth birthday at the Santa Fe Steakhouse, despite a shortage of funds. Things would be tight for a long, long time. Essentially, all of his monthly income was going to debt repayment.

"I'm not going to leave you over this, but I am going to hold you accountable for the debt you've accumulated," I had told him on the day of confrontation. I stood by that.

The morning after the birthday dinner, Earle came into the kitchen, brushing his hair. He had let it grow long again, and it hung below his shoulders, wavy and streaked with gray. He was putting it in the ponytail he had taken to wearing over the last year. He had gone through this phase before, in Lexington, after he returned to teaching full time. The ponytail went along with the motorcycle. When he moved to Texas, I suggested he cut it off because he was coming into a more conservative community. He did. But the time had come to let it grow again.

"I'd like to come to Al-Anon with you," he said.

He is so dependent. He wants to horn in on my group, my growing friendships. I am really annoyed.

"Why?" I said.

"I'm searching. Trying to find my passion." He then proceeded to ask lots of questions about how the group functioned.

That evening, he and I went to the City Café for a light dinner with the Goldwing motorcycle group. After his second and third glasses of white zin, Earle got louder.

"Did I tell you about my kidney surgery?" he said to the group, wanting to be the center. He described that experience, then went on to the ankle repair. He was clearly warming up to the telling of it all, unaware that he was losing his audience. They had heard it all before and started tuning him out. He ordered another glass of wine. I was uncomfortable, seeing it all. He did not have his hearing aids, so he missed much of the conversation and had to have things repeated.

On the way home, I drove him by the church where the Al-Anon meetings were held so he would know where to go, as I often went from work on my lunch hour. My mind was busy.

I feel like I am being manipulated somehow. This is something he sees me getting enjoyment from, so he wants to latch on. But maybe it's a hopeful sign that he's interested. I know the reality though by now. He will go a few times, make an analytical assessment, satisfy his curiosity, and stop going.

I didn't have good feelings about Earle that night, but I had to remember he was truly struggling with his life. He may have seen these meetings as a life preserver—and indeed they are, if one can reach out and hold on.

He never went.

~

Earle was sleeping more again. He would get up, eat breakfast, then sit down to watch TV, and he was out, head nodding. He woke up periodically to go to the bathroom, eat something, then it was back to the TV and dozing. He had gained more weight. His belly had become a shelf where our Chihuahua, a gift from our neighbor Mari across the street, curled up and slept. He tried to be careful of what he ate but couldn't find control. I prepared a healthy breakfast. By noon, he was off to HEB grocery store two blocks away to buy a dozen sour cream doughnuts.

"They're fresh made," he said as he walked in the door with the box. "At least I got some exercise walking down there."

It was hard to watch him struggle, but I was now fully aware that I could not help him. Still, I was sad. I worried.

~

One night, we were sitting in the living room after dinner, relaxing. Me with a book, Earle with his TV.

"Am I dying?" he asked suddenly.

"No," I said. "Why?"

"Because I'm so tired all the time."

∽

Coming into the end of 2003, I saw Earle trying to be more helpful. He said he wanted to be involved with grocery shopping. So, I included him. He did well but did not ask to go on a second trip. He was doing more around the house, helping with cleaning and dishes, which I greatly appreciated and told him so. He had been handling his own money for about a month and had done OK with that too. I was feeling in a good place.

One day when I came home from work, I noted the look on his face but did not pay too much attention. It was not Earle sitting in the recliner: It was Addict. This was my own term. I made it up. I had come to recognize the shift in quality of eye contact and facial expression. It was as though the man I loved disappeared and had been replaced by someone who could not relate.

The trigger? I had not agreed with his choice of a calendar for the new year. It wasn't a strong disagreement in my mind. He had come home with a calendar featuring border collies.

"That's nice," I said as I continued wiping off the counters. "I had been thinking about a national parks calendar, though."

"You never like anything that I get," he said, getting bullish, loud. "I don't know what I have to do to please you."

He went to the refrigerator to get the box of wine, filled his water glass, and went to his recliner. His look was angry, surly.

It's your party, not mine.

I stayed with thoughts of detachment. He was angry that I wouldn't participate in further argument.

"I'm going out to the healing room to do some work," I said, walking to the door.

"To get away from me," he responded with bitterness. "I just fucked everything up today."

New Directions

I left for my place of peace, my safe haven. The journal was waiting. It was plain, this one. I don't remember why I chose this hard-backed black book. It's about twelve inches by nine inches. I think it was all the space to write that drew me. The absence of defining features allowed only my own images to appear. Journaling became as much a sanctuary as my community of women—open, non-judging, accepting what it is mine to say.

My desk was large and comfortable. I put it together myself, one of those pressboard pieces of furniture you can buy for very little in big-box stores. The back edge was lined with objects that had meaning for me. Crystals; ceramic cups filled with pens; and a shiny piece of obsidian, black, chipped into an arrowhead shape. I had gone to Maria, a *curandera*, for a massage several years ago, and she added her own reading of my soul.

"Your husband drains you of energy," she said.

She gave me the arrowhead. "Keep this with you. It will protect you from negative energy."

Because I could see the house directly only if I got up and walked to the sliding glass door, I felt alone and safe here. I picked up my pen and began to write.

> I think I was noticing signs all week and just didn't pick up on it—an increasing need to be controlling, directive. Not in a big way, but more than it had been. What's interesting is that I have not seen this bullying, baiting behavior for a long time. Perhaps it is in relationship to my becoming stronger in my own self, my own life. The word compassion just popped into my head. And the three C's. I cannot cure this, I did not cause it, and I can't control it. Neither can he. I feel sorry for him. It must be a miserable way to live—to be so tossed by something he cannot control. But, as one of my Al-Anon friends said, I can choose not to participate in his illness. I make that choice tonight. I must make that choice every day. I must make the choice for my own health every day—this day, right now.

All was calm after that storm, and Christmas Day 2003 was a quiet, reflective day for both of us.

"Have you ever noticed Julio's toes?" I asked.

In the relaxation the quiet brought, my mind drifted to an observation that had tickled me in the past and now reappeared.

"What are you talking about?" Earle said as he put down his motorcycle magazine.

Julio and Mari were our neighbors across the street and had become good friends. Mari, short and round, was always one for new ideas. She and I had been walking buddies for years, heading for a nearby park several mornings a week for what amounted to a two-mile visit. Earle and Julio chatted over tools from time to time and admired each other's trucks. Mari's latest idea had been tai chi. She had discovered someone who held classes in McAllen two evenings a week, and we joined her and Julio in the adventure. It is always warm in that part of the world and we mostly wore shorts, T-shirts, and sandals to the class.

"So, tell me about Julio's toes," Earle said with an amused expression.

"They are so hairy," I said. "I have never seen anyone with such hairy toes. Black hair all over his toes and feet, especially his big toe. He could be a Hobbit."

"I'll have to make sure and examine them the next time I see him. Wouldn't want to miss that," he said with a smile.

We shared some laughter that felt close and loving. I was finding that I enjoyed him on a simpler level and supported his brief bursts of energy. I analyzed less and less, and so I was able to enjoy "what is" more and more. There was some magic working in me. I felt myself growing stronger and healthier.

Spring came, and the world was beautiful. The intense heat of summer was still a month or two away, birds were nesting, and it was just lovely to be outside walking amid the brilliant colors of tropical flowers. The red hibiscus I planted outside my healing room was flourishing, growing tall, heavy with flowers.

New Directions

The university was offering an Alzheimer's Quick Test to the community, as a service. I took Earle, who came willingly. It was something new to do, a chance to get out and see other people. He was always eager for that. He scored "low" with a suggestion that he seek further medical evaluation. The test evaluates parietal lobe function. This is the part of the brain concerned with reception and correlation of sensory information, which tells us about how our bodies relate to the environment. We looked at the results together.

"It just takes me time," he said.

He looked guarded, defensive.

"It might be a good idea to show this to Dr. V," I said.

"No," was his response. I honored that and let it be. I had suggested he try counseling. Dr. V had provided the name of someone she thought he might like. I thought it might help him to have someone to talk with other than me. He might gain skills and awareness. That was my hope. He went for four visits and then stopped.

"How come you stopped going?" I said.

"I'm taking a break."

He never went back.

※

I pulled the folded easel out of its corner in my healing room and set it up, placing a new 24x26 canvas on it. I was excited about painting again. It was a wonderful, creative release for me. An idea lingered from a photo that I had seen, and suddenly I was sketching a figure on the canvas, all action. What emerged on the blank canvas was a powerful African American man, head thrown back in what could be a song or a cry of pain. Colors are dark blues and browns. My joy? My pain? Remembrances of Memphis?

I stopped thinking. Now I was painting from something deep inside. The colors and shapes came of their own choosing—action-response, action-response. I worked fast, pushed by an inner energy that occupied all of me and was released through the brush as I worked. I felt alive, vibrating. The rest of the world disappeared.

I wrote too. I wrote more and more every day.

> *Where am I in all this? I am OK right now. I can allow him his path and understand that I cannot affect what someone does not want affected. It is clear that I need to take care of myself, as I am increasingly having only myself to rely on. Most things fall to me because I have the physical and mental stamina. He does not. He can no longer do odd jobs around the house. He cannot initiate the action, and if he could, would have difficulty problem-solving. I do a bit of thinking ahead, but not much as we are getting along. But I do know that I cannot do it all anymore and am becoming more OK with that. I still find myself wondering if the process that is going on now was not already begun when we met—whatever the process is.*

I was straightening up around the house on a Saturday afternoon in May when the phone rang.

"Can you come and pick me up? I laid down the bike." This was motorcycle talk for a wreck.

"Where are you?" I asked.

"At the corner of Freddy Gonzalez and Jackson."

I hurried there and found him sitting on a curb on the side of the road, cradling his right arm. He had called a motorcycle buddy who was already there with his trailer, loading Earle's bike to take it back to our house.

"I did something I know I shouldn't have," Earle said. "I was stopped at the stoplight waiting to make a left turn. The light changed and I started up. There were oil and gravel under my front wheel, and it slipped. I started to go over and put out my hand to brace the fall. I know that's the worst thing to do."

He had taken, and then taught, the motorcycle safety course.

Just then an ambulance came down the road, perhaps on the way back to home base. It stopped, and the EMTs came over and checked him. They said they could take him to the ER. I could see Edinburg

Regional Hospital from where I stood. It was no more than a quarter-mile away, but I said OK. They laid a piece of gauze over his wrist, put him in the ambulance and drove off. I followed. A week later I got a bill for $800.

Time in the ER dragged, as it always does. It was a familiar landscape now. My curiosity took over, and I asked Earle if I could try and feel energetically what was happening with his wrist. I wanted to know what broken bones felt like. He was fine with that, getting some unusual attention. I connected with my center, which happened almost instantly now after years of practice, and passed my hand over the top of his wrist, perhaps a half-inch from the surface of his skin. The energy vibration felt like a buzz saw. I was amazed at how strong that felt—a new learning.

Finally, they took an X-ray. His wrist was shattered and would need surgery, but they couldn't schedule it until the end of the following week. They gave him a temporary cast, and we went home.

> This tires me. We missed a vacation because of it. But I notice that I was not angry. I expected something like this to happen and am grateful that it is only what it is. But—I was able to say what I had to say: That is it for the motorcycles! They will be sold along with the trailer. I am in a good place today, mostly because I slept well and had a nap, too. I did nothing all day but read and pay bills, with Earle sleeping most of the time. We are just waiting now for the surgery to be done. So, I am rested. I will just take one day at a time. With his broken ankle, I spent much time being angry. This time is different. I guess I've grown.

Earle's wrist was fixed with nails, screws, and plates. But the pre-op chest X-ray showed something unusual in the right lower lobe of Earle's lung. Dr. V wanted all kinds of tests done, just in case.

The day before and the two days since were exhausting. After the surgery, I stayed with him in the hospital room. He was in a lot of pain and zonked on narcotics. He peed in his bed and the nursing staff put a diaper on him. The next day they gave him his diuretic, and he was in and out of bed every ten minutes. He was not able to handle his bulk, and I had to pull him up enough for him to come to standing. He had one huge accident all over the bathroom floor. On day three he was discharged. I was very concerned about his balance because of the pain medications.

I wait on him endlessly, it feels like. Caretaking is stressful and I find I don't handle it like I used to. It is exhausting and I can't wait to get back to work for some relief.

Almost three weeks into his healing and at last Earle was off all pain medication and independent except for the plastic bag I taped over his cast when he showered. He was moping around, looking depressed, and said, "I can't do anything."

He hasn't been doing anything for a long time.

"Let's go over to Walmart," I said, just to get him out; to give him something to do.

I tried to accept "what is," and that was Judy's Taxi Service. A sample day: I am scheduled to take Slugger, the sweet mutt that Earle adopted while he was in Lexington, to the vet to get his gums operated on, then I go down to McAllen Medical Center to get orders for needle biopsy, then I go to Edinburg Regional to pick up CT films, then I go to work, then home for lunch. Then I take Earle to RGV Regional Hospital to meet with another radiologist for consultation about the needle biopsy. Then, depending on what time it is, we go by and get Slugger, or I bring Earle back and then go get Slugger. I somehow had to get a laugh out of this—maybe hang a sign around my neck advertising a taxi service. Maybe I'd get rich. I felt removed from all of this, wondering if nothing was there. All I knew was that my life continued to revolve around Earle and his illnesses, but I must say I was doing better in dealing with it. One day at a time! And I could not control any of it. So, I just enjoyed my taxi ride.

New Directions

At the end of July, doctors were still trying to identify the mass in Earle's lung. I accompanied him to his appointment with Dr. V. After a short examination, she stood in front of him, looked him in the eye, and said, "Your weight is killing you."

Just like that.

He did not respond, and I was not sure he heard because he told me he had skipped lunch so his blood sugar wouldn't be too high when he went to see her. It was forty-nine. A lesser person would have been comatose.

That evening, after the sun went down, my healing room was cool enough to enjoy with the windows open and the breezes bringing in the night sounds, an occasional bird call and the whisper of the wind in the palms. I dropped the CD *Chant* into my old black boom box and felt the music take me into the quiet place inside.

> My husband has become someone to take care of. He is no longer a partner. His weight makes him sexually unappealing. I feel like I am separating from him more and more, and he appears not to notice. I am moving into my own space, my own selfhood, and it does not include him. It occurs to me that I have added an occupation—that of caretaker. It is a job I do—that's all. I can no longer invest any energy in rescuing or saving this person who is choosing his own path. I give him to his path and to his God. Do I love him? I love the memory of who he was and how much he has given me and taught me. Flashes of his old self still come through. But the relationship wears thin. The garment is becoming frayed and worn, held together with loose stitches and patches. I cherish all that is and was good about this man—all that we have shared. But the love is changed. I will need to think on the nature of that.

I did feel compassion for Earle. We still tried to track down the reason for the lung mass. All tests so far had come back negative, and he had no symptoms, yet the pulmonologist wanted another more invasive procedure. My husband was weighed down by this double message, and I was furious at the medical system. I was against another procedure, but Earle wanted to talk with Dr. V. And so, it just hung there for right now, an unknown.

During this time, I moved more and more into acceptance without analysis. I just responded to him where he was and protected myself when he moved into Addict. I allowed him his life—and that allowed me mine.

At the end of summer, Earle and I attended a faculty social. When we walked into the classroom in the allied health building, I heard chatter filled with gaiety and fun. I saw that long white tables had been arranged to hold the fixings for the party. I was glad Earle came because I thought it would be really nice for him to see old friends. These were people he had worked with for years.

It was the first time I had seen him with them in a while and I was taken aback. He responded to their greetings but sometimes looked as though he didn't know to whom he was talking. There was a vacant quality to his expression. His movements were slow and a little clumsy. I fixed his plate of food and brought it to him, finding myself feeling protective of him. He was pale and looked diminished in some way. It seemed like all of his cognitive processes were slowed. I was an observer now.

Bruce, our dear friend and now the dean, came over to me.

"He looks like his clock is winding down."

It was a shock to hear the words spoken.

Later that week, I knew what I needed. "Julia, this is Judy," I said on the phone. "I need Healing Touch. Would you be able to find time?"

Julia was quick to respond. "How about late this afternoon after I get things settled here at home?"

We did this for each other, calling each other for Healing Touch sessions when we most needed them.

Before she arrived, I set up my massage table so it was ready. Windows were already open. I heard the sound of birds and felt the gentle breeze.

When Julia arrived, she asked, "Is there anything in particular that you would like me to work on?"

"I trust whatever you are guided to do," I said and placed myself in her hands.

As she worked, I moved into deep relaxation. What came into awareness was a feeling of sorrow, not overwhelming, simply there, acknowledged. As the session continued, I suddenly felt unconditionally loved and cared for, through Julia's touch, her presence, but also through something beyond. It was a gift. I felt tears fill my eyes and spill from the corners, down my temples and onto the sheet covering the massage table. She continued quietly, and eventually my tears stopped.

When the session was over, I sat up and shared what I had experienced.

"I felt sorrow. It was just there, acknowledged. And I felt so loved," I said. "It was a deep and unconditional love. I feel so blessed. Thank you."

"Thank you. It was a loving experience for me too."

With the arrival of fall 2004, days were no longer as intensely hot, and I was drawn to be outdoors more. Earle was able to negotiate a position teaching one class of anatomy and physiology at the local community college. He seemed able to handle it. He knew the material and could probably teach it in his sleep—it was old learning for him. But he needed help with administrative details such as keeping track of class rolls, grading tests, and recording grades. I helped him with these things. I supported him. We worked together in his small office in the evenings, sitting close to each other at his desk amid the clutter of his multiple interests. It was comfortable—both of us in shorts and old T-shirts. It felt in a way like we were a team again.

My entire career as an occupational therapist was about problem-solving with my clients, searching for ways that would allow them the fullest function possible despite the changes illness and injury brought. That was what I was doing for my husband. The simple tasks I took on allowed him to continue to function in a way that brought learning to his students and a sense that he was still a contributing member to the world of education.

※

The mystery of the mass on Earle's lung was never really solved, but it was smaller. I mentioned to his oncologist that we had been in the Southwest the year before for three weeks and that perhaps this lung mass might be Valley Fever, a respiratory disease of the Southwest caused by fungal organisms in the soil. So, the physician, whom we both respected, started Earle on an antifungal medication. Over time, the mass shrank. We did not pursue any other ideas.

※

As we moved deeper into fall, Earle's energy was much improved.

I wonder if it's because he's teaching, because he has a bit of money to spend, or if he feels better because of the medication. Perhaps it's not important to know.

"Earle, you seem to be feeling better these days," I said one evening.

"Well, I am," he said, smiling.

It was that lovely time at the end of the day when the winds finally calmed, and the air cooled, inviting us back outside. I joined him in front of the carport where he was fiddling with some tools. I leaned up against the truck.

"Do you know what Mari told me about Julio and his escapade?"

"No, what's the latest?" he said.

Julio was a handsome fellow and had been secretly seeing someone other than his wife. Mari found out and told him quite clearly he had to find somewhere else to live. It had surprised the whole neighborhood.

"She is still boiling about him," I said. "She told me she found out the woman is undocumented. He said he wanted to help her, and boy did he help her. She said he just wanted some patch."

I watched Earle take a minute to register the meaning of the expression, then raise his eyebrows with a look of surprise. The expression slowly melted into one of faint amusement. He shrugged his shoulders.

"Keeps the neighborhood interesting, I'd say."

⁂

We seemed to be in a better place. His demands on me were fewer, and I was enjoying being around the house with him more—it was a time of simply being pleasantly together, peaceful. I knew that it was a lull and that another down time would come with depressed mood. I had learned to enjoy what was given to me.

⁂

By October, we had just moved past Earle's sixty-sixth birthday and he was sleeping a great deal again. I'd noticed it more in the past two weeks. I sensed a change in him, a subtle difference in color, further withdrawal from the world. I wondered again if there was something else I should be doing. But, if so, I just didn't know what or how.

"Dr. V scolded me again today," he said as he came in the door. "I want to start back on that cranberry juice diet. She says I have to eat right and exercise."

"OK," I said. "I'll get out that recipe book again."

The next evening, he came in with a sack full of fast food.

I saw that his balance was way off, and he got short of breath much more quickly. The pulmonologist had diagnosed restrictive lung disease. It seemed as though he wanted to move less and less. I think I would feel that way, too, if I weighed that much and was that deconditioned. I needed to talk to someone about this, find a counselor.

I saw clearly now that I must make decisions for both of us. I was now the breadwinner and the sole caretaker

I tended to bring my work home with me in my head, and it was my habit to try to slow down whirling thoughts by getting lost in busyness. I was trying to be aware of spending more time with Earle by slowing down, sitting with him after dinner to watch some TV, talking about sports. But when we did that, there was very little conversation anymore. It seemed like his life was focused around food and spending money on electronics. All else was in slow motion. Both of our lives were impacted by the state of his health. How awful it must be to slowly lose function.

"These cataracts are really interfering with watching TV," he said irritably. "Things look yellow or brownish, and sometimes I can't make out what's going on, like everything is cloudy. I need to get them fixed."

"I agree with you," I said. "It must be so frustrating. I'll make an eye appointment for you to see what can be done."

He had lost much sensation in his hands, perhaps from carpal tunnel or peripheral neuropathy. He had a slight tremor. Because he couldn't feel accurately, his movements were often clumsy. He had lost sexual function, which troubled him. I reassured him that what we had was a deep caring, and that was enough. It was as though his sensory world was diminishing and fading. He was trapped in a body that was failing him.

I was sad that he could barely hear the birdsong or the palm branches in the wind. The brilliance of the flowers was dimmed for him. All this contrasted with my world, which opened daily to the evidence of spirit and grace all around me in nature.

∴

When Mark and Michelle visited for a week in mid-December, they wanted to fill us in on all the changes in Memphis. Both were still single, living in Memphis, and engaged with their lives there. They were Earle's children, but over the years we had become close.

"All the traffic patterns have changed downtown," Mark said, "and they've enlarged the stadium."

The back-and-forth stories between them about that city and its politics flowed for a long time, with inflection, commentary, and laughter.

It was not their words but the music of their voices that lifted me up. Earle gave them both a hug and a loving hello when they came, then moved back into his recliner. He listened to them chat, but he offered very little in the way of conversation, and his expression settled into a pleasant but vacuous smile. That was how it was with us now, every day. It was such a gift to have the house filled with sound and laughter. I felt relief and support.

During their visit, I saw Earle through their eyes. It was clear that they saw him as impaired, especially with memory. I could read the nonverbal language. A sudden quietness, careful choice of words, hidden glances.

"Dad, let's straighten out all your camera equipment," Mark said one day. "You've got parts all over the place."

"OK, son. I just don't know where to start."

"Well, let's just clean off this coffee table and lay everything out here and you can tell me what goes with what."

That is what they did. With that kind of structure, Earle was able to piece things together. They worked for a half-day on that project. Mark was patient and gentle with his father. I stayed away. It was their time.

Michelle was now a clinical social worker. Her way was to tease, and Earle loved that. But I could see she was very aware of how her father had changed. There was an affirmation for me in their being there. They were seeing the changes. It was not just me.

The next day, Mark and Michelle got into Earle's office, ten hours straight, cleaning and straightening and throwing out. Earle had fallen asleep in his recliner, so I walked in and sat down with them as they worked.

"I want to tell you both how very appreciative I am of all your help and support with this," I said. "It's been so great to have you here."

Both said they were glad to be able to help out but did not add anything else.

Suddenly, my eyes filled with tears. They looked at me, questioning.

"I'm sorry, "I said. "It just occurred to me that this kind of cleaning out usually happens after a person has died." I couldn't say any more.

The first-ever snowfall on Christmas Eve fell in Edinburg, Texas on December 24, 2004. Everyone in the city was tracking the storm, and I went back and forth to the window all evening. Finally, the first flakes fell at about ten-thirty. I rushed outside to feel the big, fat flakes touch my face, suddenly realizing how much I had missed that. And then I heard a most magical sound. It was the sound of children laughing—children who had never seen snow. Tears filled my eyes at the wonder and joy their laughter carried.

"Earle, Earle," I called. "You have to come out here."

"What's going on?" he said.

"It's snowing. Come see."

He came to the door and stepped out. I saw the smile light up his face.

"Well, by golly. It is snowing," he said. "What a nice Christmas present. And look at the snow on the leaves of the plants. That is special."

We stood together for a while, arms around each other, simply enjoying. Homes were bright with Christmas lights. Neighbors were out on the streets with their children, and somewhere people were singing "Feliz Navidad." It was a holy night.

"I'm getting cold," he said.

Suddenly I remembered the grapefruit and lemons hanging ripe on the trees in the back yard.

"Oh my goodness, Earle," I said. "I've got to get that fruit picked in case there's a deep freeze tonight."

I left my husband standing in the snow as I ran inside and gathered up all the plastic grocery bags I could find. I grabbed a flashlight, ran out back, and started picking. Before the night was over, I had filled dozens of bags with ruby reds and lemons and set them, I hoped, in an artistic way, all over the living room and kitchen. They would keep for weeks, allowing me time to share the delicious fruit with friends.

After Christmas, I screwed up my courage and told Earle I was going to go with him to his next visit to Dr. V because I was concerned about his memory. He was angry, but it didn't last more than a couple of days.

I told her about the memory issues and asked for a neurological consult. She was quick to act on that; she almost looked relieved. She ordered a Doppler of his carotids and vestibular arteries and an MRI of his brain. After that, she would send a referral to a highly respected neurologist. I had been tracking Earle's behavior. His deepest sleeping was in the first half of the day, into early afternoon. He slept for about two hours, wakened for one to two hours, then nodded off again. He woke up only to go to the bathroom or to eat. His world was eat, sleep, eliminate, with a bit of football in between.

He ate huge amounts of sweets at a Christmas dinner with friends and then had huge thirst that night. I was sure his blood sugar was sky high. In the morning when I woke up, I discovered he had soaked the bed—mattress, spread, sheets. At least it hadn't gotten to my side. It was a mess. The house smelled of urine, and I ran the fans all day trying to dry it out. I felt like I was in a nursing home.

◉ ◉ ◉

The four of us sat in our customary places in Gram's casita. It was the last get-together for us in 2004, and the feeling was festive. We all brought small gifts to exchange as well as an assortment of good food to eat as we sipped our tea. Sally brought a large blue platter heaped with fresh warm tamales.

"My friend Alba made these, and they are wonderful," she said.

Julia appeared with a big bowl of guacamole with a side of chips, and Jan brought her special gingerbread cookies. I had found *buñuelos*, those crispy cinnamon and sugar covered pastries that are part of all Mexican Christmas celebrations. Warmth and comfort food and dear friends; what a wonderful way to bring the year to a close.

We all shared our Christmas activities and reviewed the last month. They all knew Earle, saw him periodically, and were aware of his slow decline over the past year. I did not need to go over it all again. I did tell them about Mark and Michelle's visit and how good that was for me as well as for him.

"I am so glad they were able to come and spend time with you, Judy," said Jan in her gentle voice. The others echoed her sentiment.

Suddenly I was in tears.

"I'm getting the feeling that we have begun the descent to an end that will come in the next few years," I managed to say.

They came to me with hugs and love and let me cry.

"We are all here for you," Sally said.

I knew they were.

CHAPTER 10

Caretaker for the Duration

We were having breakfast before going to church when I glanced at the Sunday paper. Something caught my eye.

"Earle, there's a local tour company putting together a trip to Monterrey, Mexico." I handed the paper to him. "Would you like to go? We haven't been there yet."

"Yes," he said. "I'd enjoy that. Looks like two nights and a modern tour bus. Would be fun."

We scheduled the trip for December 28-29, 2004. It was a birthday trip for me.

This big, modern, sophisticated city, with a population of over a million people, was an exciting place to be—a different world than Edinburg.

After a long first day of touring, Earle appeared a bit confused when we got back to the hotel in the evening.

"Where's the bathroom?" he said. I pointed him to it. It was right there, just off the bedroom. He went in.

"I didn't make it."

It had been a long first day, and I attributed this to fatigue and a total of six beers during the day.

"Why don't you just get into your pajamas?" I said.

"Oh, is it time to go to bed?"

"Yes," I replied.

The next day, Earle stayed on the bus most of the time while the rest of the group went into sites on the tour. He looked like he was far away, and his face was mask-like with very little expression.

The two days after our return, he slept except to eat and go to the bathroom. I was concerned. It was hard to rouse him for any length of time. I had mixed feelings. I knew it sometimes took him a couple of days to recover from exertion, but this seemed more than fatigue. I thought about taking him to the ER but chose not to, feeling I could give him better care at home. We were approaching New Year's Eve weekend, and I knew that holiday coverage in a hospital meant skeleton staff.

Then it hit me: He'd had a stroke. I noticed his walking was less stable, his finger movements were clumsier, and he was having problems finding words, mixing up words as well. I gave him his breakfast on a paper plate. He picked up the plate and put it in his mouth, showing no awareness of what he was doing. I decided to call Dr. V first thing in the morning.

> Such mixed feelings. Is this the end? Is this near the end? I fear so. My realistic occupational therapy mind tells me so. He has so many things against him and then that mass sitting in his lung. I feel so sad – so full of tears. There is love here indeed.

I called Dr. V early the next morning and she had him come to the office right away. I described the symptoms I was seeing, and she evaluated him. It did not take long.

"Earle, I'm admitting you to the hospital right now. You are having a stroke." She was in his face in her characteristic way. "I'm going to order some tests to be done as soon as you get there."

"OK," he said; no other response.

I told Earle on the way to the hospital that he could not teach this semester. The doctor and Mark, in later phone conversations, reinforced this. He seemed immensely relieved. How difficult it must have been for him to pull all of that together. But then I knew that—just didn't know why.

An MRI showed a small area of damage in the insula, an area deep in the brain. It also showed areas of deep white matter ischemia, damage from inadequate blood supply, in other areas of brain tissue.

"He has probably been having Transient Ischemic Attacks for years," Dr. V told me after looking at the test results.

"This explains so much for me about what I've been seeing for a long time," I said. "That is so helpful." I thanked her for her prompt attention to him.

We were lucky. The stroke was minor, and Earle was in the hospital for only two days. But during those two days, I had to pull him up bodily to a sitting position in bed because his balance was so poor. In doing so I bulged a disc again, as I had done in years past.

My back was very painful and sore. I could feel the stress lodge itself in there. I also had a bear of a course to teach and was not really ready. I was depressed. I had not had enough sleep and was hit with the full realization that I was now a caretaker for the duration.

As long as Earle was teaching, I could think there was more there. But each episode of illness had robbed him of more and more of his reserve, and there was not a whole lot left of the man I married. This was such a huge adjustment—huge. I wished I had time to wail and weep, but I had to get the course ready.

Over the next month, Earle did recover most of the function disrupted by the stroke. Once he was feeling better, I had some things to say.

"If you are ever hospitalized again, I cannot help you the way I have been," I told him. "I hurt my back and caused damage to my shoulder in trying to pull you up. The doctor has prescribed physical therapy for me."

"I'm so sorry, sweetheart. I wish I could do something to help you, and I do understand," he said, taking my hands in his. "All of this scares me."

"I know it does. We just have to take one day at a time."

I went to see Dr. V for my own check-up, and she found no problems. I told her about feeling tired and draggy, and she said, "You have to take care of yourself."

Don't I know?

"Does Earle have Alzheimer's?" I said.

"No," she said. "This is vascular dementia. "

Cold hard words.

> It was not supposed to be this way, but then who are we to think we can know all that will come our way? And so, I will enjoy what I can of this man for as long as I can and try to remember to take care of myself.

I had a nice phone call with Roxie, an old friend who was the chair of another occupational therapy program. I filled her in on events with Earle, whom she had met some years before.

"How difficult it is to get outside of the context of ourselves in order to see what we need to do to take care of ourselves," she said.

Very true words. *How do we step out of our skins, our gut, our lives, to see what it is we need?*

Early spring 2005. The weather was lovely, and the scent of citrus blossoms was heavy in the air. My hard-backed black journal was on my desk, waiting for me. It was a long time since I had written. I turned on my desk light, a leftover from Mary's college days, and took up my pen.

> How do I handle this? I am married, but alone. I am married, but single. I live a married life, but in many ways must learn to live a single life. I have a life partner, but he is not a partner. He is indeed still a companion. And I do love him.

The reality is we are moving into a new phase in our lives. I cannot deny that I am married to someone who is quite ill but wants to live. There is courage there. Or is it will? He is a strong-willed person. And I am in this life with him. I cannot run away from that reality. We have to slug it out, come what may.

March brought a welcome break, a trip to Vera Cruz, Mexico, with my sister, Jane. She flew down to take the weeklong excursion with me. It was so very relaxing being away from work and away from home. I needed that. We talked a bit about our lives—not too much—but enough.

"It was hard for me to let myself go on this trip," I said to her as the bus sped along. "I'm not comfortable leaving him. He fell last week coming out of Staples. Just went off the curb. It took two men to get him up. He told me he was afraid he was having another stroke, and I had to reassure him that he is not."

"Judy, you arranged for people to come in and check on him, didn't you? Just enjoy."

This was said in her no-nonsense, matter-of-fact way. My sister, the voice of reason. I could honestly say to her, in another conversation, that—YES—Earle was a burden. He was indeed the elephant in the living room. It felt good to voice this. It felt good to hear the words out loud.

☙ ☙ ☙

Earle was on a sex kick again. He wanted me to be his sex kitten, to perform.

"I just got home from work," I told him. "It would help if you would just hold me or rub my shoulders for a bit. What I need is some romance, some transition. I need you to reach out and rub my back or head or shoulders, or even a hug to move me into a different place."

He complained and tried to guilt me.

"Maybe some time for intimacy might happen next year," he said with a heavy, "poor me" tone.

I argued with him about that. I felt as though I were an object. His approach was without romance or sensitivity—just getting his fantasies met. He had nothing to do but sit at home and watch TV and conjure up horny thoughts. I was the breadwinner, working full time, with associated stresses. And I came home to someone who weighed three hundred pounds and was frankly no longer physically attractive to me. I enjoyed being with him. I enjoyed the companionship, and there were times when we had fun.

We'd had this conversation before. All this sex stuff was only in his head when he'd been drinking. There was no real connection with me as a person. It was so very lonely.

As I knew would happen, he fell asleep soon after dinner and eventually toddled off to bed.

಄ ಄ ಄

Our first real go-round about the alimony happened during our first year in Lexington. Earle's divorce settlement included, among other things, an alimony payment of a thousand dollars a month to his former wife, which would end if she remarried. She never did.

"Earle, you have been faithfully paying your alimony for six years," I had said then. "Can you not go back to your lawyer with a request to revisit this? It would be incredibly helpful to us if that went away."

"The truth is I'm afraid," he had said. "I'm afraid if we open this back up, she will ask for even more. I just can't do it. She is so angry."

I could see the fear on his face. His worry was authentic. I was angry, too, but I did some hard talking to myself. *This is not my business. It is an agreement he made with another person. I knew that when we married. It's just what is. I have to let it go.*

I did let it go. His decision was part of the package that I married.

⁂

But now, in 2005, I brought it up again. This time it was not a question.

"When Katie called the other night, she was filling me in on all kinds of chatter about people I had known in Memphis when I was still married to her dad," I said. "One of the people she mentioned is a lawyer. I remember meeting her. I'm going to get in touch with her and begin a legal exploration toward getting your alimony eliminated or reduced."

"I don't want to do that," he said. "She might want more."

"Earle, there is no more to be got," I said. "Basically, all of your income is going toward your debt payments, and you are a sick man. I don't think there is a judge anywhere that could be pushed to bleed you for more. I'm going ahead with this."

~⁂~

Earle found a gym after doing much research, as he put it. He went three days in a row, and he truly seemed better since the stroke ended his teaching responsibilities. Perhaps there would be a clear ending at last to that part of his life. I think he was also buoyed up by the possibility of being free of alimony. That remained to be seen. He continued to process language and action slowly, but he did process.

~⁂~

The legal effort took six months, requiring a retainer that came out of my savings, but the final verdict was that the alimony payment could be reduced by half. Every little bit was helpful, even five hundred dollars a month. Earle ran through that first month's extra money like he was a child in a toy store. My love and compassion disappeared.

"Earle. Beginning next month, I am going to take $400 of that $500 to apply to things we need to get done around the house and bills that need to be paid."

He was very angry, but I really didn't care.

~⁂~

That same evening, he was still angry.

"That is my money," he said loudly. "You don't care about what I need."

He stomped around the house, grumbling.

"Everything is your way. Maybe one day I'll get a dollar or two to get a magazine."

It felt abusive. I changed the subject and left for my healing room.

"It seems we didn't finish the conversation," he said later when I came back in.

"It felt abusive to me, and I will not take part in that," I said evenly.

He returned to ranting anyway.

"Get over it," I said.

All of this was relatively civil. I was just straightforward.

He had been drinking lots of wine, and I went to bed at about eleven or eleven-thirty. I noticed on some level that he came to bed after that. Then something woke me at twelve-thirty or so. Earle was not in bed, and I thought he had gone to the bathroom, so I got up, as I had to go as well. I walked around the bed, and there he was on the floor, a mountain of flesh in urine-soaked Depends with one leg caught under the bed and his head between a dog kennel and the wastebasket.

"Get up," I said. "I can't pick you up. You're going to have to do it yourself."

It took him ten minutes to untangle himself and to figure out how to get up. I walked him to the bathroom because he was staggering, drunk as a skunk. Then I handed him a clean Depends to put on and walked him back to bed. Pitiful. Pissed me off.

I woke up the next morning, not having enough sleep and feeling as though I had been battered. He woke up pleasant as can be. Dr. Jekyll and Mr. Hyde. After breakfast, I told him exactly how I felt. He listened with no comment.

Today, I did not love this man. I wanted to be away from him. But I was much better about being as honest as I knew how to be. Not mincing any words or leaving anything out. I vowed to spend more time at work.

It was quiet now. He had not had any wine since the incident. Like it all never happened. The energy in our house was so dead—so heavy. Earle talked very little. Said he didn't feel well and complained of shortness of breath being worse and aching in his side and back.

I had to get out of the house. Re-runs of *Law and Order Special Victims Unit* were blaring. I could lip-synch them. Earle was sipping wine. Again, I retreated to my wonderful room and my book of solace.

It has been a clear, spectacular day. The smell of blossoms, lemon, grapefruit, and orange fills the air. It is quiet, peaceful. There are many birds now. Our kiskadees are back, and a pair of mourning doves as well this year. Sparrows, red-wing blackbirds, Inca doves, mockingbirds. My spirit friends. How I love it. Only a month until the end of the semester and then the stress will be less. I have vacations to look forward to. I chose to stay home this afternoon after teaching in the morning.

I'm feeling the impact of aging, and the changes seem to be moving more quickly. Vision issues. Changes in joints—hip soreness when I walk. I am angry about this now but know I will adapt. Again, the thought. How do I want to live the years left to me?

Finally, the semester was over. It was early May 2005 and Earle and I set off for a one-week vacation at a time-share in Sedona, Arizona. I had fallen in love with the place when we took our longer trip to the Southwest two years before and looked forward to the change. In Sedona, we walked through the tourist shops a bit, and that was all that Earle had energy for. He became short of breath quickly, and I thought it might be the altitude. In any case, he was content sitting in the room watching sports on TV. I got out and hiked and sunned by the pool. It was great.

A Native American gentleman called Thomas came to the resort once a week to talk about his culture and native ways. His tribe was Klamath-Modoc. The presentation included his wife, who was Lakota Sioux, and his two daughters, who danced traditional dances. I spoke to him afterward.

"I have always been drawn to Native American culture, and I practice a kind of healing that sounds much like what you described in your talk." I explained a bit more about Healing Touch.

He listened carefully.

"You are an Indian in white skin," he said. "I'm going to have a sweat lodge ceremony at my house in Cornville tomorrow night. You are welcome to come."

"I would very much like to," I said.

※

The drive to Cornville and Thomas's house did not take long. His wife had given me directions the evening before. It was still light, and I found the one-story beige brick home, in a small development, with no problem. The yard was dusty with a scatter of cactus, creosote bush, and sage. I noticed ants were very busy as I walked along the path to the front door. One of his daughters answered my knock and invited me into a spacious living room ringed by long black leather couches. A large deer hide covered one wall. There were painted figures and animals on it. When I asked what it was, Thomas's daughter told me it was the story of her father's life. Drums, a pair of longhorn antlers, and paintings with a western theme decorated other walls. I sat on one of the couches.

I was surprised that others were already gathered; a small Japanese tour group and a couple of other white people. We waited quietly for Thomas, who finally arrived from another commitment, dressed in jeans, cowboy boots, and a black shirt. His black hair was shoulder length. He said a pleasant hello, then sat down in a chair and played his flute. The music was gentle, hypnotic, inviting—a meditation. It drew us in. After about ten or fifteen minutes of playing he stopped.

"I welcome you to my home. I would like to hear from each of you a little bit about yourself and what you want from this experience."

We began, one by one.

"My husband is a very sick man, and I am concerned about him," I told him when it was my turn. "I am also a healer and have done study in this area."

When we all said what we needed to say, Thomas talked to us all generally.

"There is a balance between the spiritual and corporeal worlds, and it is very important to maintain that balance," he began. "Our ancestors lived with balance between the intuitive and the intellectual—heart and mind. Our corporeal world has shifted all to the mind, and so we are like babies, learning to walk with our intuitive gifts. Before we go to the sweat lodge, my wife will explain what that will be like, while I go and prepare."

His wife entered.

"The sweat lodge for us is a way to purify ourselves physically and spiritually. We believe that we sweat away illness, unhappiness, and negativity and invite in helping spirits with prayer and song," she said. "You must take off anything with metal in it before you enter. This includes rings, glasses, or any clothing that might contain metal. Women may not take part if they are having their period because during that time they are open to the earth, able to receive that wisdom. My older daughter will not take part today for that reason. Women must also wear long dresses or skirts."

I looked down at my jeans, and back to her, questioning.

"I have some extra dresses for those who might need them," she said with a smile.

"The opening of the lodge is low, and you will have to enter on your hands and knees. Crawl around to the back as far as you can go, then sit with legs stretched out in front of you. I have towels for those who did not bring them."

When we were ready, we were shown out into the back yard, in the middle of which was a large, canvas-covered dome-shaped structure. Next to it was an outdoor fire pit in which large round stones, about the size of a man's head, were heating in the flames. A man tended the fire, focused on his task.

I crawled through the opening and then around to find my place. The floor was packed earth and in the center was another fire pit. Thomas was already there along with his younger daughter and another native. His wife joined when we were all inside.

Then the fire keeper lifted the flap on the doorway and passed in a pitchfork, on which were placed four glowing red stones. Thomas helped to place these in the pit, using a strong stick. The firekeeper returned with more and more stones until the pit was filled with red-hot rocks, and then the flap over the opening closed.

"There are four rounds," Thomas explained. "The first is an invocation where we call in the presence of sacred powers. In the second round, we all talk and pray out loud at the same time, telling the spirits what we are grateful for and what we are asking of them. In the third round, there may be messages for people, and in the fourth, we say prayers of thanks for all we have received."

Then Thomas, his daughter, wife, and the other native man began to sing and chant as they played drums. Thomas sprinkled water on the rocks. Steam rose. He periodically dropped in small quantities of herbs, which lit and then rose in sparks within the smoke. The chanting drew me into its rhythm. We were all sweating.

It was time for round two, and everyone called out their gratitude and prayers. Thomas encouraged us all to speak loudly so the spirits and powers would hear. The space felt holy to me. The only light was from the glow of the rocks, and the air was filled with the smoke and scent of the herbs and special plants, mixed with steam. The sound of our voices raised together unified us.

During round three, there was more singing and chanting, and then Thomas began to speak. He had general messages for the whole group that echoed his earlier message of connecting with our intuitive selves within the larger world we live in. He then had specific messages for two people only. I was one.

"You must live with integrity as a healer," he said directly to me. "You must also know that many of your peers will not understand and will stand in opposition to you—even family. You must have faith in your path and must protect yourself as a healer."

Then he added, "You must always keep one stone for yourself. That is your medicine. Medicine can be in many forms, birdsong, a smile, a quiet place, a hawk that you see in the sky. But you must always keep one stone for yourself. As for your husband, it is not your role to determine his path in this life."

His voice was strong, and his words were arrows into my heart. They mingled with the sweat, the red glow, and the scent of sage.

"We are like leaves floating down a stream, sometimes sailing smooth, sometimes getting caught," he said. "Each leaf makes its own journey. You must have faith that your husband will be healed as he is meant to be healed. You must turn away from him and walk away, praying the prayer of faith for him, and in doing that—in that act—you will let him go and help him heal."

I was stunned.

This is what I came to Sedona for.

The fourth round came. Again, there was singing and chanting to the drums as the rocks continued to steam. We were directed to give thanks to spirit for all that we received. All voices responded, each in our own language. It felt like completion, closure.

The flap was raised, and cool air rushed in. Slowly, we moved and one by one crawled out into the cool night air. A man gave me his hand to steady me as I stood up. I moved toward the house feeling that I had in some way been fundamentally changed.

Inside we found that his wife had prepared tacos—enough for an army. When I asked, the night before, what the charge would be for the sweat lodge, I was told there was no charge.

"Just bring some food to share with everyone."

I had brought a watermelon, and it complemented the meal. I also found a way to leave some money even though the ceremony was clearly an offering to us.

When I returned to the time-share, I found Earle in bed, sick. He had a fever and diarrhea, which he had not been able to clean up. So, I found the cleaning supplies and set to the task. It took a while, but I finally got my husband and the bathroom cleaned up. I felt sorry for him that he felt so bad, but I was removed from the task, still feeling the spell of the evening. When I finally lay down and closed my eyes, I saw plants, rocks, and flowers as I had seen them on my walk that morning. But the colors were intensified and almost liquid, as though there were a layer of pure clear water over them. It was beautiful.

The next morning, Earle looked much better and was able to eat a light breakfast. We had a quiet morning. I talked about the sweat lodge experience and told him what Thomas had said.

"Earle, that is what I am going to do. I am going to turn my back and walk away, praying in faith that you will be healed as you are meant to be healed."

He looked startled but said nothing.

"You will be healed as you are meant to be healed," I repeated.

We sat comfortably for the rest of the morning and into the early afternoon, talking when we wanted to, being quiet when we needed to. It felt very peaceful. The doors and windows were closed, but all of a sudden I felt a wind rush through the room even though nothing moved, and I knew that the virus had left and he was well.

I was eager to tell my Healing Touch group about this vacation and all that had happened. Fortunately, we had a meeting set for the week after I got back. There we were in Gram's casita, and we went through the telling of what had gone on in our lives since the last visit. During my sharing time, I told them about the sweat lodge experience.

"Oh, Judy," said Jan. "That must have been so powerful. How special."

Sally and Julia joined in with similar responses. They were fully present with me, wanting to hear everything.

"There was one other thing that came out of that for me," I said. "I felt that I had a life shift. Teacher, occupational therapist, mother, wife—those are things that I do. But what I am is a healer. I have always been a healer. I have unusual sensitivities and gifts that were not recognized by my family group, and so I felt unseen."

My dear community of women listened and nodded with understanding.

"I received affirmation of myself as a healer in the sweat lodge and was able to voice that awareness out loud, in the presence of others, for the first time in my life."

We talked on for quite a while about how we saw ourselves, knitting the bonds between us more tightly.

As we entered more deeply into fall, I took full responsibility. Somehow, I encouraged purchase of a border collie puppy, and it was driving me crazy. I truly love animals. Earle had been obsessing about this breed for years, and I guess I needed novelty as well.

Earle had the truck cleaned to go pick up the pup, expecting instant bonding, which happened for me.

"They always go to you," he said accusingly.

I would wait and see how long his interest in this animal, who we named Slick, lasted. Earle's binge with the gym was about over. My motive was to get him up and moving a bit more, and that had happened minimally. I didn't know if this would work with him, although our home was much livelier. But the pup's energy level got to me. He badly needed training; I felt overwhelmed.

Katie called during this time and we had a wonderful talk—a brief respite. Soon after, there was a call from Mary as well. My daughters have become my friends and have their own special wisdom. Their calls were so welcome, filled with catching me up about their lives. I could share as well. They brought me energy.

Despite the excitement over the new pet, Earle became depressed again.

"Why don't we go over to the schoolyard and do some work with Slick?" I said. I just needed to get something moving. I had connected with a trainer who was teaching us to work with this dog, although I was the only one doing the training, of course.

"OK," he said. "It's a nice evening. Let me get my training outfit on."

He reappeared after about ten minutes, dressed in black gym shorts, white tennis shoes and tube socks, and a white T-shirt with the name of the gym on it. His beard was full and almost all white. A blue sweatband held his long gray hair back from his face. He looked huge. I noticed dark circles under his eyes.

We went to the schoolyard, and I moved through the skills Slick had learned. It was a pleasant place. Earle sat on a bench, watched, and talked about wanting to work with Slick but took no action toward that. I resigned myself to the fact that I would do most of the physical work with the pets as Earle's energy was no match for theirs. The animals were the life in our house.

A few days later we had a fight. I came home from work tired, opened the front door, and walked in to see a pile of dog poop on the tile floor. Earle was supposed to take Slick out. I lost it. I yelled at Earle with frustration, anger, and blaming. Later I apologized and got back negativism and guilt trips. I lost it again, yelled, and carried on. It was a long time coming, I guess. Then I sat out back and had a good cry.

> This is what I've got. This man, this house, this job, in this state. This is it. No more illusions, wishes, fantasies. Perhaps no more dreams. I find myself not wanting to initiate new things. Just continue with what is already begun and be content with that.

In mid-July, Earle was back in the hospital, this time for four days with diagnoses of cellulitis, a urinary tract infection, and a blood ammonia level of 107.

"Does he drink?" the internist on duty asked.

"Yes," I answered truthfully, then asked what blood ammonia levels meant.

"There can be many causes, but in your husband's case, I suspect liver failure," he said. "Ammonia is toxic to the brain. If the liver cannot function, it does not clear the ammonia from the system."

"What would happen then?" I said.

"Symptoms can be confusion, lethargy, muscle weakness, decreased attention, depression, bipolar disorder, tremors, sleep disturbance, delirium, and even coma. We can treat this with a medication called Lactulose. It will bring down the ammonia level, and I have already given him a dose. But he will have to stop drinking."

This event really scared Earle. Something got through—he did not have anything to drink after the episode, nor did I think he would again. He checked his blood sugar every morning. Dr. V had another MRI done because she wanted to see if he had had another CVA, which I knew he hadn't, but she needed to do her thing. Her report to him was that there has been an increase in the atrophy of his brain since he had his stroke six months ago. So, there indeed was some process happening.

Out to eat one evening, I was talking about work and mentioned a faculty member in social work who had died.

"Social work? Is that a program in your college?" Earle said.

Just three years ago he was involved with that department in weekly meetings to work through their accreditation process. I had to mention other faculty members' names before it came clear for him.

> It occurred to me this morning that his brain has done the work it was meant to do in this lifetime, and now is done. And that's OK. I can accept that. Earle is physiologically old now, but he has contributed much to many people. He was a warrior who can no longer fight and hunt, but he is still a person in this world, this life, and in our home.

At the end of summer, we had a truly wonderful week in Orlando. It was very restful. I went with no expectation except to do just that. Earle and I reconnected with each other in a way that we had not in a very long time. Perhaps not since we were dating, before life piled up on us. He laughed at my preoccupation with a raccoon on the grounds of the resort that was adept at begging for food.

"I enjoy seeing you happy," he said. "It's fun to watch."

I talked to him about my work, as I used to, many, many years ago. He was always my sounding board, my mentor.

"I have lost my passion for occupational therapy," I said. "I keep working because it builds up retirement and because we could not survive without my salary."

"Do you feel trapped?" he said. He was always able to look for the essence of what I was talking about.

"No, I don't," I said truthfully. "But I don't feel excitement either."

In our conversation, I found that I was grateful for the time I had left with him.

❧

The summer heat had left, and the lovely weather that October brings arrived. Earle's ammonia levels continued to be high and he continued on Lactulose, which caused significant diarrhea. His sleeping increased, and his times out and about decreased. But he was happy as could be now that we had built a woodworking shop. He had talked about that as a wish for years. I had my healing room, a place of my own, so I understood his need. We had space in the yard, and I found an old life insurance policy of mine that was not worth much but was enough to pay for the construction of the woodshop. So, we went ahead. He could buy little things and putter. I knew it would never be used properly, but he was very happy with it, and so, it was worth the investment.

By my letting him go, I had in effect freed myself. Our relationship was better. His sense of humor continued. I accepted that he did the best he could. There was very little physical help with the house, but whatever he contributed was something.

❧

We had a small metal storage unit in the back yard that was rusting, so we decided to get rid of it. In cleaning it out, I found a box full of photo albums and brought them into the house. We sat down together to look at them.

"Do you remember that trip to Destin?" I asked. "And the one to Reelfoot Lake north of Memphis?"

"Oh yes. Those were wonderful times," he said with a smile.

As we started going through the photos, I was shocked. They were taken shortly before we were married. I saw that I was beautiful. I radiated energy and happiness. I was voluptuous, looking younger than my forty years. And Earle, a different body in a different time. He radiated vigor. His face was very sensual. Those pictures were twenty-five years old. It seemed like a day and a lifetime all in one.

I looked at us today. How different we were. Bodies changed; energy changed. I was not sure what I radiated now.

"Do you think I'm still attractive?" I asked him.

"You are as beautiful as the day we met," he said, meaning it, and he gave me a rare spontaneous hug.

Later that week, I took some time for myself to connect with Sally. She filled me in about her trip to Tibet with New Age author Gregg Braden earlier that year, while we enjoyed a wonderful two-hour lunch. The experience sounded amazing. Then, something in that conversation sparked a memory of the trip to Sedona and something else Thomas had said.

"We must consider everything that we do," he said. "Don't just throw water out but spill it gently, giving thanks to Mother Earth when you do so."

"I've been trying to remember to act on that," I said. "The pouring of the water as I empty the dog's water bowl has come to feel like a sacred act to me."

"Purposeful," Sally said.

"That's what it is, a purposeful blessing," I said. "I would like to learn how to do that with many other aspects of my life. I do many things that have purpose to be sure, but I don't bring purposeful intention to what I do."

"That is pretty profound and something to really think about," Sally said. "We'll have to stay connected with each other as to how we are doing."

I wanted Earle's sixty-seventh birthday to be a good day for him, and it was. The sweetness in our relationship continued. I felt in love with him but now on a more spiritual level. He kept changing as well. He got mad at me about something or other the other day, and for the first time in twenty-four years he did not rant and rave but talked it out! Thank you, God. What a gift.

But I felt that our time together was tenuous now.

"I'm noticing over this last month that I have more problems with balance and with using my hands in a coordinated way," he said one evening.

"I've noticed that too," I said.

His anger of a few days ago gave him clarity. When he had a specific goal, it sharpened his mind. Otherwise, memory was an issue. However, I felt that our love was growing deeper.

∽

Still, apart from that, I was depressed. I could not deny that feeling anymore. A few days before Thanksgiving I talked to Katie and to other friends about it, and they reassured me that it was OK to accept medication to help with this. I talked with Dr. V about it.

"You are always 'on'," she said. "At work with work and with Earle at home."

"I never thought of it that way," I said. "I feel like I don't even remember what it feels like to rest. I know Earle's condition will continue to worsen."

"Yes, it will," she said.

"It's so hard to watch, this slow, painfully slow decline. And the conditions fluctuate daily."

"I'm going to prescribe an antidepressant for you, and I suggest you get counseling as well," she said.

Then she was off to see another patient.

I think I have been depressed on and off for a long time. Trying hard, and most of the time successfully, to fight it off. But I just can't do it anymore. I am tired and I am soon to be sixty-four, and I don't like getting old.

I continued to try to sort out my thoughts about work. I was basically putting in my time, for the income, and for increasing my retirement and Social Security benefits. Earle's debt would not be paid off until the end of 2007—two more years. I worked all day and came home to someone who just sat. He did go to a movie with me last week but missed much of the dialogue because of his hearing. He fell asleep in his chair that evening at about eight forty-five. The time available for conversation was about one hour.

There was life, but it was very different. No stimulation. I was bored. I needed change, and my partner could not engage with me anymore on that level. I was concerned about our debt—that weighed on me. I did a great deal of traveling that was work-related in the past year. It helped me to keep up a certain level of energy and excitement, but it was all self-push. I cannot push anymore. Earle has actually gotten a bit better with good medical management. He looks better. So, this truly may go on for years. I have had to take care of myself, and I feel like I don't know how anymore.

Mark and Michelle visited again, just before Christmas 2005. It was good to see them, and I felt their support. I knew they cared about their dad and about me. The weather was cloudy and dreary, but despite that, we had a fun trip over the bridge to Mexico. We did not stay long and walked slowly, at Earle's pace, but it was enjoyable to spend that time together.

One evening as Earle dozed, I had some time to talk with Mark and Michelle about how my life was beginning to change.

"I have a grant-funded opportunity to go to a Myofascial Release workshop in February in Arizona. It would be very beneficial for me, both in teaching and for my interest in the healing arts, but it's ten days long. I don't feel that I can leave your dad alone for that length of time," I said. "He seems more short of breath lately."

Mark offered to come stay with his father if I got the grant, and I thanked him. I was so relieved.

We kept on with fluctuations; sometimes good days, sometimes not so good. Earle started to have occasional falls. They usually happened in the living room as he got in and out of his recliner. His balance and coordination were declining.

One evening, I was in the kitchen preparing dinner and heard the thump.

"I fell," I heard him say.

"Well, let's see what we can do," I said calmly as I came into the room. He was on the floor near the recliner. This event was not something that concerned me. I had been a practicing clinician and guided many people through movements despite bodies that did not work well. And so, I guided him.

"First, can you roll over and push up onto your hands and knees?" I stood next to him and stabilized him while he did this.

"OK, good," I said. "Now I'm going to get a dining chair because it's more stable." I did that and placed it close to his head.

"Now, look up at the chair." He did that. "I want you to put first one hand and then the other on the seat of the chair. When you are ready, pull yourself up and move your knees closer to the chair." He completed that.

"OK. Now just push yourself up into standing." I stood by to guard him as he slowly stood up.

"Take a second to get your balance, and then you can walk over to the recliner."

I had a sudden remembrance of how patient he had been those many long years ago in Kentucky when he guided me through the process of baiting my hook and learning how to fish. *We have been guides for each other.*

After a few other such falls, I felt it was time to deal with my safety concerns.

"I think we should look into Life Alert," I said. "It's a wristband or necklace that you can wear to signal someone if you need help. I'm worried that if you fall sometime and I'm not here, that you could lie here for a long time. It wouldn't be fun."

His eyes brightened. A new gadget.

"I think I would like the wristband," he said. "Do they come in colors?"

゛゜

Suddenly, it was close to Thanksgiving. I was finalizing my tenure document, three inches thick, which was enormously stressful for me. I did not have a PhD, and our program was a clinical program. I had no idea whether the layers of committees sitting judgment, or the provost, would approve me for tenure, and so I gave that to God as well.

During this time, I found Gretchen, a good counselor and a woman whom I would like as a friend. Her message was consistent: be with what is, day by day, feel the feelings as they come up, and don't run—just be with whatever is there, and feel compassion for the enormity of the central issue: loss. The writings of Pema Chödrön were especially helpful during this time, as were my dear and increasingly precious family and friends.

I slowly moved along with preparatory thinking about retirement. Asking questions, looking at finances. It was time to talk with our long-time friend, Bruce.

"Bruce, I want to retire as chair of the program as of August 2007," I said. "I just can't do it anymore. My role as caretaker is becoming more predominant. Earle's memory issues are significant. I am his temporal center, and I am very tired."

"You have paid your dues," he said with genuine sympathy. He was grieving the loss of his friend as well.

I feel scared sometimes that he may not live much longer.
However, I had that thought many years ago, and here we are.

CHAPTER 11

The Ending

The call came on December 18, 2005. My eighty-seven-year-old mother, who lived in Pennsylvania, was hospitalized with congestive heart failure. This had happened a number of times before; an emergency trip to the hospital by ambulance, stabilization, and then home to carry on as usual. The question that always lingered was, "Will she make it this time?"

This time she did. Earle and I had already planned a Christmas trip to visit her. I was glad it worked out that way. She would be back home by the time we got there.

My sister, Jane, was already at Mom's house when the ambulance brought her home. Living only two and a half hours away, she was the one who got called first. Mary and Chris drove down from Binghamton for a day. They now had two children, five-year-old Wyatt and two-year-old Chloe. Both little ones were delightful, and they cheered us all. There was good talk time with Jane and Mary while Earle and Mom were dozing in their chairs. We caught up on how our lives were going. Earle seemed content with the visiting and was socially appropriate, joining in the conversation from time to time. He enjoyed my mother.

After we returned to Texas, I had a long phone call with Katie, in Maine, as well. With her busy work schedule and our unpredictable days in Allentown, there had been no time for in-depth conversation. Katie and her partner, Jen, were both nurse practitioners now, and so she wanted all the medical details about Mom.

"How do you think she's doing?" she said.

"Well, she's tired from the hospitalization, but her spirits are good," I said. "She filled us in on the latest gossip at Luthercrest. Who was taking too much food out of the dining room, who had fallen, and which man had gone into a certain woman's apartment and not come out until the morning. She's sharp as a tack."

Luthercrest was the retirement community that my mother had lived in for twenty years. It had become her village. She had her own one-bedroom apartment and lived independently, although there were times when that seemed to be getting more problematic as both her vision and heart were failing.

"How is Earle doing?" Katie said.

"Well, there are good days and not-so-good days, but overall he is holding his own right now."

"I know it's hard for you, Mom. You've got that program to run, and I know he's difficult. I care about you. Please take care of yourself."

"I will," I said.

The women in my life—my family of women—nourished me.

My other well of nourishment, my Healing Touch friends, had gotten together earlier in the month for our Christmas get-together. It was always so good to reconnect. We shared baked goods, candies, and stories and filled everyone in about our holiday plans. We had even dressed up a bit for the occasion, with long skirts and bright blouses.

"I want to spend a weekend at this place," said Sally, handing out brochures. "And if anyone would like to join in, please do."

The brochure described a silent retreat center called Lebh Shomea, about an hour and a half north of Edinburg, near Sarita, Texas.

"I think I really need this," I said.

No one else was interested, but Sally and I planned a weekend as soon as the holidays were over.

⁂

We rode together to Lebh Shomea. I had arranged for people to look in on Earle, and off we went into a new experience. We would spend Friday and Saturday night and return on Sunday late afternoon. I had packed a small bag and my journal.

"This place is beautiful," I said as we drove onto the grounds.

"Oh, it sure is," Sally said in agreement. "Everything is peaceful and seems so well cared for."

We found our way to a small bungalow with a sign above the door that said 'check-in,' walked in through a pleasantly creaking screen door, and were greeted kindly by the person on duty.

"You will both be in the Big House," she said, "but on different floors. Here are your keys."

The Big House was a beautiful, large, and spacious three-story building with a white stucco exterior and red tile roof. There was a bell tower at the very peak of the roof and tall palm trees grew around the big circular driveway. We were told at check-in it had been the home of Sarita Kennedy East, who willed it to the Missionary Oblates of Mary Immaculata in gratitude for all they had done for the spiritual life of early settlers and their families in that part of Texas.

I found my room easily. It was large and bright with the sunshine of the day. I saw simplicity: white walls, a single bed, a brown dresser, a small but adequate desk and desk chair, and a larger brown easy chair. A small bathroom with a narrow shower stall opened off the bedroom. The only wall decoration was a cross.

A white binder on the desk gave the rules as well as maps of walking trails. The Oblates were a contemplative-eremitical community, and the House of Prayer was dedicated to silent listening of the heart within contemplative prayer. There were, in fact, a number of hermits living quiet and permanent lives on the grounds of this thousand-acre estate.

TAPESTRY

The only time talking was allowed was on Sunday during lunch. If there was some communication that needed to happen, it was to be whispered. The only request was that those visiting take part in a daily morning service, at seven, in the beautiful, modern, light-filled chapel on the grounds.

> I am at Lebh Shomea House of Prayer. I feel I could be happy here for a very long time—so quiet. Animals everywhere. Deer wandering around or just lying there. They don't even move. A parade of turkeys tonight—I think a hundred—oh, the sound of turkey feet walking down the path made me laugh. Then a walk in the moonlight—such stars. Coyotes howling, and earlier, at sunset, dozens of turkey vultures circling, then coming to roost in the tops of the palm trees. I walked a lot—I became aware of how tight my body was—holding tension. When I became aware I could let it go. I am not yet relaxed, but it will come.

I continued exploring the grounds the next day. I identified a walking trail called the Wilderness Walk and took it on. It took me two and a half hours to complete, winding through thick brush and sand dunes covered with buffalo grass.

I roamed the 30,000-volume library in the Big House, amazed at the diversity of readings, and found a small chapel and solarium tucked away in smaller rooms.

> When I laid down last night and closed my eyes what flashed before me, like a streaming video, were faces—face after face—all kinds. And I knew they were images of me in past/other lives.
>
> On my walk this morning I understand that this part of my life is my desert walk—shifting sands—work so hard there is no time to think of anything except the exertion of putting one foot in front of the other. But I also understand that I am loved. Loved by Spirit/God/Universe.

The Ending

I found other paths, explored the Cowboy Cemetery on the grounds, saw an armadillo and small bands of javelina, and discovered grapevines everywhere. I cut many of those to take home. *These will make great frames for dreamcatchers.*

Sally and I occasionally saw each other on the grounds and respected the rule of silence except for one time in passing.

"Isn't this an amazing place?" she whispered, blue eyes sparkling, face joyful and animated.

"Oh, yes," I agreed.

> It took me until today, but I have reached peace and stillness inside. The day was beautiful, all in peace and quiet. Outside all day, in nature, in healing. Am understanding that all those things I label problems in my mind will not go away—they are part of life. This has been a breakthrough weekend. How rigid and driven I have been especially over the past year. I made myself separate—not part of humanity—the human condition. My life and the issues I face are no different from anyone else on the face of this beautiful earth. What a relief to let go and be real. Gretchen said to just allow the depression to dissolve. I like that word, dissolve.

Julia, Jan, Sally, and I met for our group get-together again. As always, I looked forward to these times. We knew each other so well and were connected in many ways beyond our healing group. Julia and her husband were congregants at St. Matthew's, and we saw each other weekly. Jan and I worked in the same building at the university and had developed an original research study focused on Healing Touch. We worked on committees together and saw each other almost daily. Sally and I went antique shopping, to the movies, and out to lunch fairly often. We four had been meeting together for six years, and the bedrock of our relationship had become trust, honesty, respect, and love.

"I really want to talk about my time at Lebh Shomea," I said. "I feel like enormous shifts have happened, and it would help me to process what I'm feeling."

"Please do," said Jan. "I've been eager to hear."

The others were equally as encouraging.

"I've become suddenly aware of how stuck, how shut down I've been, caught in patterns—habitual patterns," I began. "I'm finding it scary to peek out, to think about making the choice to stop and take the risk of personal change."

"Oh my," said Julia. "I can't even go there right now. I think if I looked at all that and tried to do something different, I would need big-time therapy. Maybe one day I'll get there."

"I know what you mean," Sally joined in. "I do keep looking at that in terms of Jack's and my relationship. It's so hard to try to negotiate change when the other person is not ready."

"I made Earle the repository of my depression," I continued, not able to stop now. "But my depression is not about him at all. It's about how I've viewed my life. It's about acceptance of myself, and my life as it is. I think I've known this on some level for a while, but now I feel like I'm beginning to know it in my soul."

"Wow," Jan said. "What a huge awareness for you."

"I used to want to run away from what I perceived as difficulty," I continued on. "It's a very strong pull and a very scary thought to stop running."

Everyone listened and was present with support. They were my soul sisters.

※

I returned home to a quiet house. Earle had dozed off in his recliner and, amazingly, the TV was turned off. I went out to my healing room. The evening was warm and lovely, and the yard glowed under a full moon. Grasshoppers and peepers sang their songs, and I heard an occasional night bird calling out. A nice, peaceful time. My journal awaited.

Things are good right now. I sit with the awareness of having to change some life patterns—not sure yet how to do that except that I must be much kinder and gentler with myself. Earle is really good right now. His ammonia level is way down, so

The Ending

glimmers of his old self appear, including his humor, which is helpful to me. It is nice.

Awareness of how emotionally shut down I have been perhaps beginning as long ago as the Lexington years. Awareness of how I have put up a protective wall in the face of Earle's mood swings. And how very hard I have been on myself.

Springtime came, and the end of the semester was close. One Saturday morning, as we sat in the living room having a second cup of coffee, I started a conversation.

"Earle, I'd like to talk about what kind of plan each of us might have for after we die. Neither of us is getting any younger, and I think we should think about this so we can tell our kids."

"Well, that's an interesting subject for a Saturday morning," he said with a smile. "Can you be more specific? Are you talking, for example, about a flaming boat pushed out into the Nile?" He was enjoying this.

"I'm talking about burial plans," I said. "I would like to be cremated and have my ashes sprinkled into a deep valley that I once visited in western North Carolina. It was so beautiful. How about you? Any thoughts?"

He took a few moments to think about this and then said in a clear, firm voice, "I want to be cremated and have my ashes spread over three bodies of water." He looked pleased at the thought.

"What three bodies of water?" I said, surprised.

"One is the Gulf of Mexico."

There is a list coming. I can hear the professorial tone. His lectures were always organized, linked, and made information clear as a bell.

"It's a place where I have always wanted to sail, and it's so close. It connects with my memories of summers in Gulf Shores, Alabama, with my Uncle Bud."

"OK," I said, my attention drifting to the dust motes floating in the ray of sunshine streaming through the patio door.

"Second is H Lake in Arkansas." His voice was strong and without doubt.

"Well, I guess I could find it if I needed to," I said, not sure about this developing plan.

I knew his history with H Lake only through his telling of stories of his many fishing trips there with his buddies, Jim and Larry, during the time he worked for the university in Memphis. Those trips were before I knew him, but I had gotten to know his friends well after our marriage.

Before I could even finish processing this, I heard, "Number three is the Buffalo River in Arkansas." Again, a clear pronouncement. "I have always loved that river. It's wonderful for canoeing, and so beautiful."

We had canoed together on that river in our early days, and it was indeed beautiful. I knew how much he loved it.

"Is that it?" I said. "No more bodies of water?"

"No, I think that will do it," he said with a smile. He knew what he wanted.

"OK," I said.

An agreement was made.

At the end of May, when my classes were over, we took a week and went to a time-share in Branson, Missouri—a lovely resort town filled with country-western and hillbilly shows. Earle loved it all. I knew how to pace activities so he could keep up and not get over-tired, and he did well. But we were in a different place, surrounded by lots of other people. I suddenly saw him as others might see him. I noticed a pallor to his skin. He moved almost in slow motion, and there were circles under his eyes now. When he was tired, he seemed to deflate and sink into himself.

I wonder how much more time we have.

Our summer passed quietly. We had made some decisions to take simple actions to spruce up the house, including having laminate flooring put in throughout; there were people in and out to help with that. It was a good feeling to plan something together. I noticed that I felt an absence of the need to be involved in healing work right now and had stopped accepting new Healing Touch clients, although I continued with a full schedule at the university.

The Ending

In early September, I took a ten-day block of time to be with my mother in Pennsylvania. Her condition was deteriorating, and I needed to be there. My sister could come for only a few days at a time because she was working, but my work situation sometimes allowed me longer periods. Friends would look in on Earle.

I did need to be with Mom. Her physical body was wearing out. I simply spent time with her, preparing small meals or going to the dining room with her, moving into her rhythm of activity and naps. Sometimes she wanted to talk, and I was able to be present, just hearing. Mary drove down for a day with her children, and Jane and her husband, Mick, came for a day as well. We moved easily in and out of each other's space as people who love each other do.

"It means so much for me to see those children, and to see you," she said.

"It means so much for me to be able to be here, too, Mom," I replied. "It doesn't happen very often. I live so far away."

Mom would sometimes talk about her childhood, stories I had heard many times.

"I was the middle one. Louise was the pretty one. Robert was the first son, and Oscar was the favorite son."

I became newly aware of how, in a way, she never left her childhood perceptions, despite all she had accomplished in her life. She saw herself as less than in so many ways. Jane and I would try and point this out, reflect back to her all she had done. She could never hear it. It was almost as if the pain of what it would be like for her to change was greater than the pain of staying where she was.

I left with a feeling of peace. Mom was tired and ready to go, I think. She was aware of her failing endurance and the limits of her vision. In our long times of quiet, just being, I felt that I entered her presence, connected with the essence of her. No words were spoken or needed; just a peaceful being together, mother and daughter, loving.

On my flight home, my mind drifted to Earle. How different from Mom he was. In her decline, she seemed fully present, accepting and at peace. My husband seemed to have no awareness of how ill he was or that he might not live a full lifetime.

～

Early in October, I gave myself the gift of another weekend at Lebh Shomea. In January it had been cool, even chilly in the mornings and evenings. This time of year, it was hot, muggy, and buggy. But I continued with my walks and drank in the silence and peace of the place. I did ask for a visit with Father Kelly, one of three resident Oblates.

I walked down the leafy path to his small wooden cottage, set well back from other buildings; one room and a screened porch. That was his home. I knocked on the screen door and he invited me in and motioned to a chair on the tiny porch. I settled in and immediately felt drawn to this man; lean, spare in build with thinning gray hair. He looked like he might be in his mid-seventies. But what caught me was his warm, gentle, and loving face.

How beautiful a presence he is. It is as though in living this simple life, for all of his life, he has become his essence.

We were both distracted by a movement in the woods. I followed his glance and saw a beautiful buck, standing quietly.

"They visit me here," he said softly. "Now, what would you like to talk about?"

I talked a bit about Earle, but also found I wanted to talk about Healing Touch and how it felt when I connected with the energy of other people.

"Your work is spiritual, charismatic," he said. "Keep doing it. It will never fit within a church because a church is an organization. Your healing work and the church are on two different levels and will never meet."

That had never occurred to me. I had much to process.

"I thank you so much for seeing me," I said as our time drew to a close. "You have given me affirmation as well as much to think about." We parted with a warm hug.

～

Thanksgiving Day 2006, as we took our meal at a local hotel, I filled Earle in on a new development.

"My friend Cynthia has nominated me for Fellow in the American Occupational Therapy Association. I'm really excited about that. It's a very rigorous evaluation process and a prestigious honor. Only a few people are selected each year."

"That's wonderful," he replied. "You've worked so hard all of your life. You deserve to be recognized."

His response was warming. He was always supportive of me. I could always count on him for that.

The fabulous weather continued for a few days after Thanksgiving. One morning I gathered up Slick and we were off for a walk. I went along one of my favorite routes, past the dancing mesquite trees. These were my favorite trees in this sub-tropical part of Texas. They were not very tall, and their trunks grew in curves and twists that only they could imagine as they adapted to the growth around them. The wood is beautiful, dense, and red hued. It is wonderful wood for fires of all kinds, but especially for grilling chicken and ribs. I looked forward to my two special mesquites on this walk. They grew side by side like siblings, or friends, or lovers wrapping around each other. Their trunks moved in a dance that changed and shifted as one walked by. Experiencing them was a meditation.

Slick and I were gone for about forty-five minutes.

"Earle," I called out when we came back. There was no answer. I did a quick look around, and then I saw him. He was on his back on the small concrete patio just outside the sliding glass door off the living room.

I opened the door and walked out.

"Well, what happened?" I said calmly. I no longer felt alarm with events such as these. I became my professional self: observe, assess, evaluate, problem solve.

"I came out to see what the dogs were doing," he said. "Then I bent over to pick something up from the grass and suddenly I'm here."

It was a six-inch drop from the patio to the grass.

"How did you end up on your back?"

I started to assess his physical situation. His legs were on the grass, the rest of him on the concrete. It appeared to me that he must have fallen backward.

"I just don't remember," he said with a bemused expression.

It was clear that, in that position, much like a turtle on its back, he had been unable to roll his bulk over into any other position. I was grateful it was early morning; the sun was still gentle, and I had not been gone very long.

He had full ability to move. I carefully pulled him up into a sitting position, and then after a minute or two, up to a stand and we went inside.

X-rays taken the next day showed a compression fracture of L2, which was very painful for Earle. There was no specific treatment. It just had to heal itself. The next three weeks were pure exhausting chaos for me. Compounding the situation was poor pain control initially, then a course of Vicodin, which eased the pain but made him loony and unsafe. Then followed horrendous incontinence caused by Lactulose. I spent a week scooping poop off the floor. Dr. V had referred us some months before to Dr. O, a gastroenterologist, for management of his liver disease. Thanks to this kind and competent doctor, medication adjustment was finally worked out, and at last, the diarrhea came under better control. I was grateful that this was between semesters, as Earle needed constant guarding when he was up and moving around.

December 21, 2006, was our twenty-fifth wedding anniversary, and I truly felt blue. It was a rainy and cloudy day. Earle was not aware except for a brief moment. His memory had gotten worse. I felt so very tired, and I was disappointed at what came of that day. I truly wanted a celebration for us both.

"Earle, it's our anniversary today. Would you like to do something special?"

"Oh, it is?" he said, searching for the memory. "I'd like to go to Taco Bell for a beef taco."

I cried as I drove him to get a beef taco. He unwrapped it and started to eat as I drove back home, totally immersed. I cried for a while after we got home. I just had to. It had always been a special day to him, with a card, a gift, and a bouquet of flowers for me. Not long after we got home,

The Ending

a white truck with "Florist" written on the side in big red letters pulled into the driveway. I went out to meet the driver who was climbing out.

"Judy Bowen?" he said.

"Yes," I answered.

"These are for you." He brought out a huge spray of flowers. The card was signed: Mary and Chris, Katie and Jen. It said, "Happy Anniversary, with love." What wonderful medicine for my soul. Tears flowed again.

~

Earle and I went to the Christmas Eve service at St. Matthew's, a celebration that we both loved, filled with color and music, joy and friends. Earle was pleasant and responsive to our friends who knew of his fall. He had wanted to come even though it exhausted him.

People were helpful and considerate. Earle wore a back brace most of the time now. He said it helped ease the pain a bit, but it limited him on the hard wooden seats of the pews.

"I know what we can do," said the young priest whose name also happened to be Earle. He went up to the altar area, picked up the big brown bishop's chair with the blue needlepoint cushion, and brought it to the center aisle beside our pew.

"There you go. The arms will help you get up and down."

"Oh, thank you. I really appreciate that," said my husband as he moved himself out of the pew and into the bishop's chair.

I sat in quietness during that service and suddenly understood that I had spiritually separated from Earle and was now on my own path, walking forward. I had a visual image of being separate from him and it felt like peace. I would care for him and love him for all he had given me, and I continued to learn—about both of us.

~

My sixty-fifth birthday, on December 28, passed just like the anniversary. I said happy birthday to myself as I walked Slick in the morning. Earle did not remember and looked a bit confused when I reminded him. It was a beautiful morning—bright and still and quiet. I decided to stay in gratitude, and for the whole walk I listed all that I had to be grateful for in prayer. But by that evening I was back in the depths. I cried and cried. I could find no solace for myself anywhere. New Year's Eve came and went. The blues just hung there.

Earle continued in his dependency.

"Earle, I know your back hurts and it doesn't feel good to move," I said one morning. "But I really need your help with things like taking your dishes to the sink or picking up after yourself."

"OK," he said. "I'll try."

To his credit, he did.

※

Early in January 2007, the letter came. I could barely contain myself.

"Earle," do you remember that award that Cynthia was going to nominate me for?"

"Yes, I think so," he said, looking up at me from his woodworking magazine.

"Well, I'm going to get that award, in two categories. They'll be presented to me at our national professional conference in St. Louis in April. I am so excited."

"Wonderful," he said. "You certainly deserve that honor. I know how hard you've worked."

I did feel honored, acknowledged, and affirmed by my peers. I had accomplished much and had done all of that in the face of enormous challenge: living with Earle and growing out of co-dependency—growing toward my own health.

※

The spring semester began. I was already tired, feeling like I could never get away from unending requests.

I invited a new faculty member, Marcy, over to dinner one evening. She and Earle hit it off. He was still charismatic and engaging, even though the luster was dimmed. I wondered if she would be willing to stay with Earle for a few days. I wanted to visit Lebh Shomea again, needing retreat. I asked Earle about this.

"Would it be OK if I went on a retreat again? I could ask Marcy to come and stay here with you. She might even cook."

"Oh, that would be great," he said with enthusiasm.

The Ending

When I saw Marcy again at work, I broached the subject.

"Marcy," I said. "Would you be interested in staying at my house for a weekend? I'd like to get away on a retreat and I can't leave Earle alone."

"Oh, I'd love to," she said.

And so, I had a reprieve.

⁓

Spring, my favorite time. The air was filled with the songs of birds that came with mating season, and the scent of citrus blossoms again filled every corner of my healing room. My journal had become the person I talked to, my personal friend to whom I could say anything. And so, I talked.

> Earle is cognitively better than he has been in a long, long, time, and that is great for him. But physically he is so debilitated. There have been several more falls. We've had a month of chiropractic and now a month to come of physical therapy. Hopefully he will gain some strength. I continue to be always the one to run and fetch and bring. I am depressed. I am not in a good place at all. I don't want to work. I don't want to be a handmaiden. I am so burned out. What I would really like is six months by myself. I am hoping these upcoming trips will help. To Orlando in three weeks and then soon after to St. Louis. The reality is that because Earle is getting good care by me, he may live another ten years. I am just in a bad place. I don't like it and feel stuck.

Earle fell again at the very end of March. He was in acute back pain again and slept in the recliner in the living room because it was too painful for him to lie down in the bed. I could not do it anymore. Home health services were now part of our family; he had areas of skin breakdown on his bottom because of the skin stresses of constantly sitting. Skin breakdown justified a nurse, according to insurance guidelines, and his balance issues justified physical therapy. Both were a psychological help to both of us. I also used the services of the Area Agency on Aging for coverage if I had to be away. They sent a pleasant volunteer whom Earle liked and who was content to wait on him.

There were times I thought he looked like many nursing home clients I had seen. That, in fact, was the reality. I distanced myself somehow. I saw him as a client/patient, and that helped. I would be going to Disney World with Mary, Chris, and the kids for a promised week at a timeshare. I had to. Somehow, I would arrange coverage.

Earle will most likely never drive or travel again. I think he is at another level of chronic illness—always lower. A tiring road.

The physical therapist and I decided a rolling walker would be the best choice for my husband. He would not have to lift it up and forward with each step. It rolled smoothly on the laminate floors we had put in earlier in the summer. He learned to use it quickly, and it gave him much more stability when he was walking around the house. I worried about that as he had taken to being awake for much of the night, restless.

"Well, good morning, sweetheart. You've been busy," I remarked as I came into the living room one morning late in March. Somehow, Earle had managed to rearrange many of the lighter pieces of furniture despite his painful back and poor coordination. "Looks like you've had a busy night."

He looked at me. Face a bit flushed. Eyes a bit brighter than usual.

"What were you trying to do?" I asked as gently as possible.

"Well, I don't know. I just had to do it," he replied.

"Why don't you rest a while now?"

That evening we were sitting in the living room. I was reading, and he was watching TV.

"You have to get the windshield fixed quickly. It's dangerous the way it is," he said with sudden urgency.

I had no idea what he was talking about.

"The windshield is fine," I said. "I just drove home from work."

"No, the windshield is shattered," he said, this time a little louder. He was giving an order.

The Ending

I got up, walked over to the front door, and looked out at the car. It was fine. I had a choice—to argue or to understand.

"OK, I'll call the garage in the morning and get it taken care of."

He relaxed.

~

On Good Friday, April 3, 2007, I was teaching a class when the department secretary opened the door and rushed to me.

"I'm sorry to disturb you, but EMS is on the way to your house. They got a call that your husband fell."

"Folks, I'm sorry, but I'm going to have to cut class short," I said. "There is something at home I have to take care of."

I was glad that Earle apparently remembered his Life Alert bracelet.

I got there at about the same time as the ambulance, went in before the two big men who were coming toward the door, and put Slick out back. Earle was on the floor, his back against the wall separating the kitchen from the living room and his feet up against the back of the recliner. I could never have gotten him up.

"OK, sir, we're going to pick you up," one of the men said as they got on either side of him, leaning over to get their hands under his arms.

"Wait," I said. "He's got two compression fractures in his back."

"Ma'am, we've got to get him up." In what seemed like a second they had pulled him to his feet. We walked him to the recliner, allowing him to ease down into it.

I thanked them for their help, and they left.

"What happened?" I asked.

"I don't know," he said. "I just fell."

Again, the bemused expression on his face.

I called Dr. O that afternoon and described what was happening: the hallucinating about the windshield, the restlessness, the falls.

"You need to get him to the hospital," he said. "You cannot handle him anymore at home."

I felt relieved. Someone was affirming what I already knew.

I called Dr. V and told her of my conversation with Dr. O.

"I'll arrange for a direct admit," she said. "Take him over there now."

I thought I could walk him to the pickup with his walker, get him in, and then deliver him to the hospital. We started out the front door, but then he just collapsed—just sat down on the step and could not get up.

"Well, Earle, I guess it's time for you to push the Life Alert button again."

EMS came quickly. They got him up on a gurney and into the ambulance. Earle was sitting up, conversational, friendly, and alert. The novelty seemed to stimulate him. He was the center of it all.

I watched as the admissions clerk fed Earle's medical directive into the slot that scanned it into the hospital computer system. It contained the Do Not Resuscitate directive, which was his wish as we formulated our directives. I knew the end was near.

His room was on the medical floor. Diagnosis: acute hepatic encephalopathy. He relaxed into the hospital bed, back positioned to give him support. He had not been able to lie down since last November. I imagined he must have been grateful to be taken care of in a place where equipment and medication allowed him comfort. He did not verbalize this, as he was busy chatting with and charming the hospital staff. The 1 milligram of morphine eased him and let him sleep.

He had tried so hard to be independent at home, but it just wasn't enough, for either of us. Much better that he was here. For the future? Rehabilitation center, skilled nursing facility? Not home. I decided to talk with the hospital social worker in the morning about placement in long-term care. He needed the care of a full staff of professionals, and I had said that to him. I was just so tired. Once he was settled, I went home.

I was back and forth for a week, running home to tend to the dogs and to the university to try to keep up with events there, and then coming back to the hospital until all quieted down for the night.

A week later, when I arrived at the hospital, Earle was nowhere to be found. "Where is my husband? He is not in his room," I asked the nurse on duty. I was alarmed.

The Ending

"Oh, he has been moved to the rehab floor," she said, giving me his room number.

I supposed that Dr. V felt he was medically stable, or the insurance company did, so he was transferred to the rehabilitation unit. I found him in his new room and gave him a hug.

"Well, I see you have new digs," I said. "What will you be doing here?"

"I am having therapy," he said. "They take me there and I have a physical therapist." That was all the information he could provide.

The room was essentially the same as all hospital rooms—impersonal, utilitarian. But this room had a dresser with a big mirror, and it warmed the place up a bit.

I went to the rehab gym and met the therapist involved with him.

"What are your goals for him?" I asked.

"We're working on safety in transferring from bed to chair and back, as well as progression to using the walker again." Familiar and appropriate goals.

Earle showed some progress for the first few days, then was transferred back to the medical floor.

"I don't understand," I said to his therapist. "The nurse just told me he had been moved." I was angry at the news. I still hoped for a return of the man I once knew.

"His balance is beyond what we are able to handle," the therapist said, direct and honest. "He has no awareness of his body, and he is so big and so confused that he is a danger both to himself and to staff. He can't follow directions. We can't handle him here."

The words of the physical therapist shredded the last bits of hope I had for the man that I loved. My objective mind knew exactly what the therapist was saying. But I could now clearly see that Earle was disoriented, unconnected to what was happening to his mind and body, lost to me. One of the last coherent things he said to me was while I was helping him get a shirt on. He was about to be moved back to the medical floor and was sitting in a wheelchair. He could see himself in the mirror.

"Will you comb my hair?" he asked. I did, running the brush gently through his shoulder-length, wavy gray hair.

"I am not a quitter," he said, looking at us both in the mirror. It was a statement, blue eyes bright.

"No, you are not," I said with conviction.

Tears welled up in my eyes. It was indeed the way he lived his life. Despite all that came his way, he never quit.

I slept on a sleeper chair next to him for a few nights, as he was restless all night long and often jerked violently, crying out, "I'm falling, I'm falling." He was truly terrified. I got up and soothed and reassured him when this happened but got no sleep for myself. I decided there was nothing I was doing for him that the hospital staff was not already doing. He was incontinent and pulled sheets and covers off, so they had to be in his room often, changing him and settling him down. I remembered Thomas's directive to keep one medicine stone for myself, and so I started sleeping at home again and went back and forth from home to work to hospital.

"Dr. V will be in this morning to see you," I said.

"Oh," he said, alarmed. "Where is my back brace? I've got to have my back brace on. She'll yell at me."

"I think she will know you don't need it right now."

I was not sure he registered what I was saying.

I heard the stiletto heels in the hallway before she walked in, red hair resplendent.

She stopped at the foot of the bed and stood for a few seconds looking at him.

"He's been hallucinating," I said.

There was a small clothing cabinet in the room with open shelving at the top, holding an extra blanket or two.

"Earle," she said. "What do you see up there?" She pointed to the blankets on the shelves.

The Ending

"Why, I see cats," he said, pointing into the air. "They are all over." He was smiling.

The doctor looked at me.

"This is progressive," she said, brutally direct, and left the room to see other patients.

Later that afternoon, as Earle was resting, I talked with him about the people who had come to visit. Easter had come and gone, and friends had come, bringing him little gifts and cards. He had tried to stay awake and social for them.

"Get that over there," he suddenly said, pointing to a stuffed purple Easter bunny. I gave it to him.

"Now come here," he said, beckoning with his finger. I leaned over and he reached up and wiped my cheek with it, very gently, as though he saw something there.

"Thank you," I said. It felt like a kiss.

> I am in a whirlwind, a skid, a slide. In these last three weeks, Earle has become very ill. He lies there in the hospital so terribly confused, so terribly agitated, in some other world. I feel so bad for him—neither of us comprehending what is happening in a way. It's all been so fast. I don't know what to do. Each day he slides deeper into the confusion and is so very frightened sometimes. He would not wish to live like this. I don't know what to do. Do I bring him home? I want to love him, care for him. But my rational mind says I cannot. He needs to be in a place where he is cared for by professionals. I have not been able to cry except for a few tears here and there. I am just getting by—have things walled back. So hard to see him like this. I don't know what to do.

When I walked into his room after work on the evening of Friday the thirteenth, ten days after his admission, he barely recognized me. He responded to simple questions, but according to his nurse, he was no longer eating or drinking. He stared off into some other place. He was jerking a lot, calling out sometimes. I could see that he was leaving.

I called Sally, Jan, and Julia that afternoon, letting them know what was happening with him. I needed support. I needed my friends. Jan was able to come by for a few minutes after work. She stood quiet and still next to me; a loving presence.

"It's time to communicate with him on a spiritual level," she said simply.

A nurse came in.

"The Lactulose is no longer lowering his ammonia level," the nurse said. A statement of fact—the medication was no longer helping.

Before I left to go home, I leaned over the bed, touched his arm, and talked to him.

"Earle, it's OK to go. I love you." I saw no sign of response, but it was his spirit I was talking to, and I trusted that I was heard.

That night, with intention, I energetically connected with his spirit and told him again that it was OK to go. Later I learned that Jan and Sally had done the same.

I came in and spent the next morning, Saturday, April fourteenth, with him. Earle no longer recognized me or acknowledged anything in this world. His eyes stared, and he was more agitated.

His nurse came in. I noticed she was young and had a softness about her.

"I would like to make sure there is a Do Not Resuscitate order on his chart." A statement I said resolutely.

"I'll ask the doctor when he comes in," she said, glancing at Earle.

I went home for lunch, then to Lowe's to pay a bill, and got back to the hospital at about one-thirty or so. There was a major change. Earle was uncontrollably violent. He had pulled out his IV, was thrashing and shouting out loudly almost constantly. He was in extreme agitation, pulling off covers. He had nothing on except a diaper. Eyes staring. There were nurses in the room, and they all seemed unnerved. His nurse told me they had just given him a shot of Haldol, which is contraindicated in liver failure, but I accepted and understood their need.

"Is the DNR order on his chart?" I asked his nurse.

"The doctor refused to write it. He said he was just covering for the weekend and was not the primary physician."

I was furious.

"His medical directive is in the hospital computer system. I saw the admissions clerk enter it."

"I couldn't find it," she said, looking very uncomfortable.

My entire being felt like pulsing anger. This was about my husband, so I snapped.

"Then go find someone who is computer literate—it is under durable." I was almost shouting now, not caring about hurting someone's feelings.

Earle was so agitated with his shouting and fighting that he began to hyperventilate. His color paled and the pulse oximeter clipped to his finger showed that his blood oxygen level had dropped into the seventies. His nurse called respiratory therapy and two men came.

"We need to intubate," said the man in the white scrubs.

"No!" Now I was loud, firm, clear. "He would not want to live like this. Can't you see that he is trying to die?"

The respiratory therapist in the blue scrubs was more empathetic. I could see the caring in his eyes. He heard me.

"What the wife wishes we will do," he said to his partner. "We can put the full-face mask on him," which they did, and his color began to improve.

Just then, Earle's nurse came back into the room.

"The doctor has written the DNR order."

I felt so relieved. I thought: *She is, too.*

I noticed that the Haldol started to work. Earle suddenly became very quiet. Then his blood pressure started dropping—down to 53/35. Blue scrubs and white scrubs dropped the head of his bed and raised his feet. They brought in the red crash cart and attached leads to him to measure heart rate.

"I want to let him go," I said. Loud and clear.

"If we do nothing, he will go," said the one in blue scrubs in a soft but direct way, looking at me.

"That's what I want."

The respiratory therapists left. There was a sweet nurse's aide in the room for all of this, who was with Earle when he was first admitted. They had connected and enjoyed each other.

"Why don't they listen? You are so strong," she said. Then she left.

Another man walked into the room.

"I am Doctor Martin," he announced. The almost-absent physician for the weekend. "I can put some medication in his IV that will raise his blood pressure. Do you want that?"

"No!"

"His heart is slowing, and his lungs will fill with fluid."

"No," I said again.

He left the room.

※

Finally, Earle and I are alone. He is very quiet, and I am so grateful for the Haldol, which has given him peace. I get most of my body up on the head of his bed and put one hand on his chest; with the other, I stroke his head. I talk to him the entire time, telling him I love him and that it is OK to go. I feel his skin, the feel and temperature of his body, the feel of the hairs on his chest, acutely aware it will be the last time. He is very quiet and still. I have to consciously and deliberately push through something deep inside me in order to let him go. We have perhaps thirty minutes and, slowly, he dies. He just stops breathing. I watch the monitor flatline.

The time of dying is one of such love and intimacy—much deeper than in the time of living. Quiet; holy; a passing.

I loved him so much.

※

When he was gone, I called the nursing staff. They came in, unhooked everything. I gave them the name of the funeral home and they called. Then they washed him. After that, I sat with him for another hour until

The Ending

the mortician arrived. I helped move him to the gurney. It was good. I touched him as I waited and felt him cool. He was only sixty-eight.

֎ ֎ ֎

The memorial service was held on April 20, 2007, to allow family and friends who lived some distance away time to get there. People brought food, enough to feed an army. Friends came by.

A few days before the memorial service, there was a knock on my door. When I opened it, there stood Julia, tall and lanky, with loving energy.

"I'm so sorry. I didn't know. We were out of town."

"Please come in," I said, so glad to see her.

We sat on the couch, and I talked for a long time, filling her in. Finally done, I found myself laying my head on her shoulder, and the tears came. Her arm went around me, sheltering, accepting, loving.

St. Matthew's Episcopal Church was packed. There were people from the university, from the congregation, from the community. It was such an outpouring of love for Earle and me both. The custom in that church was to allow time for anyone who would like to speak about the departed to do so.

First to speak was Jim, who had worked with and for Earle for many, many years in Memphis. He told funny stories about their fishing days and then gave an example of Earle's administrative skill.

"The university administration determined that all programs and departments needed to cut their budgets by ten percent. Earle took all of us, representing the fifteen subgroups that fell under his charge, into a conference room. We all came out an hour later in complete agreement as to how that would happen. That was the kind of leader he was."

Next was his brother. I had no idea he was going to speak and was so touched. He talked about his respect and love for his older brother and about their growing up together in Alabama. Not normally a demonstrative man in my experience of him, he clearly was in pain at his loss, tears welling up in his eyes.

The next was a woman who had been involved in the Education for Ministry program and spoke highly of Earle's spiritual leadership, good humor, and keen mind during the time he was involved.

And finally, Melinda, who had been a student of his in the nurse practitioner program at the university, came forward.

"He is here. He is in me because he was my teacher, and he is in all of the others he has taught."

My tears came and did not stop. I gave up trying to hold them back. They flowed even more as, walking out of the church at the end of the service, I saw my students gathered in the back. They had all come.

―∻―

Over the next few days, visitors and family from out of town left. Mary, Katie, Mark, and Michelle lingered, helping to begin sorting through Earle's belongings, clearing out bags full of things he bought but never opened and returning them to stores to claim refunds. The total amounted to several hundred dollars.

It was so good to feel surrounded by their loving care, but finally they needed to return to family and work.

What now?

―∻―

I return often to my sacred space, my place of peace, my journal, my friend. On this particular late-spring day, the dogs are resting on the cool patio just outside the sliding screen door of the healing room. Birds are singing with their own joyfulness. The wonderful scents of the Rio Grande Valley, distant sea breeze, and flowers fill the air. I know the sweet little green anoles are nearby, eager for a passing spider or insect, and butterflies of a variety of colors move through the beams of sunlight. All are angels, spirit friends to me. They bring their own grace.

> *I have no idea how the future will unfold. I have a hole in my heart. It will take a long time to heal. I miss Earle terribly, but there is some relief in talking with him.*
>
> *I have tuned into his spirit twice now and both times I heard him lovingly say in his Alabama drawl, "You'll be just fine. You'll*

The Ending

be just fine." I can see his smile, his blue eyes, gaze direct and clear. I can hear the support and love in his voice, always there.

I emailed the American Occupational Therapy Association that I would not be able to attend the awards ceremony in which I would be named a fellow. It was the Saturday night immediately following the memorial service. Family and friends were still in town. I could have gone for an overnight. The flight to St. Louis was not long. But I did not have the emotional energy, I told myself. I felt a commitment to these people who meant so much to us both.

I know exactly what Earle would have said were he still alive. "Judy, of course you have got to go. This is the crowning moment for you for a lifetime of work. Just go."

But he was not here. My choice lingers as a regret. Something for me to reflect on along with many other things.

The experts say that no major decisions should be made for a year following a loss. I believe and respect that. I have time to begin to understand what my path will be with some things already set, such as another year of teaching before I retire. I have my community of women who I know will walk my path with me. Our children are there for me, caring, supportive. I have Lebh Shomea, another place of peace and connection with spirit.

I trust all will be well.

CHAPTER 12

FLY AWAY

"You have escaped the cage. Your wings are stretched out. Now, fly." —Rumi[2]

It was important to me to honor the last agreement I made with my husband, the agreement about the three bodies of water. It took me four months to move forward with this.

Being a compulsive sort, I decided that Earle's ashes needed to be distributed evenly, so one afternoon at the end of summer 2007, I got out the box sent by the funeral home, marveling again at how heavy it was. With the curiosity of a health-care professional, I opened the inner bag and stuck my hand in. I was surprised that the ashes felt grainy and rather harsh, not at all like beach sand, which I had imagined.

I pulled out a box of gallon-sized zipper-lock bags with pink closures, got my one-cup measure, and proceeded to measure his ashes, cup by cup, into the three bags, so as to have equal distribution. Earle would have laughed, our children would have laughed, and now I laughed. But such was my need then to make sure his wish was granted, giving equal importance to all three sites.

The first was easy. Paul and Letty were members of St. Matthew's and had known us both for a long time. They had enjoyed Earle, as everyone had. And they had a twenty-six-foot sailboat. I approached Paul one day and asked if he would help in meeting Earle's request about the distribution of his ashes.

"Of course," he said. "Let me talk to Letty about a day and time that would work, and I'll get back to you. We'll have to go out beyond the reef, as we're not supposed to scatter remains. But we'll make it work."

And so, Earle's first request was set in motion. I asked my friends if I could include Sally, Jan, and Julia, as well as Julia's husband, in the excursion.

"Of course," said Paul. "They're all good friends."

We met at the boat slip on South Padre Island, and everyone piled in with me and my pink-zippered baggie. It was a beautiful, sunny summer day as we sailed out beyond the reef into turquoise-blue water, sunlight reflecting off gentle waves.

"What I would like is for each of you to take a handful or two of Earle's ashes, say your own personal farewell in any form you wish, and then throw the ashes into the water," I said as Paul maneuvered the boat so ashes would not blow back on us.

One by one, each person took a handful, moved to the end of the boat, into his or her own private space, and said their goodbye. It was a burial service. I felt like Earle was there, totally enjoying it. There were some ashes left when they were finished, and I just took the bag and emptied the remainder into the Gulf, wishing him blessings on his journey. Then Letty disappeared into the small cabin below and emerged with several bottles of chilled white wine and plastic cups.

"It's time to celebrate," she said as she began pouring.

"Oh, Letty," I said. "I am so touched. How thoughtful of you." I certainly knew Letty from her involvement in St. Matthew's but had not been as close to her as to some other congregants. I was touched deeply by her innate kindness and her understanding of what was needed at this moment. The gesture was perfect. I suddenly wondered how many more people there were, in my circle of acquaintance, who understood my needs and held me in their loving thoughts.

We all found places on the deck, stretched out, and enjoyed the wine, the sunshine, and each other's company.

"Earle would have totally loved this," said Sally. "A very fitting celebration."

"You know, I really enjoyed all that he brought to St. Matthew's, said Julia's husband. "He made a lot of good suggestions. Had creative ideas."

"And he was a lot of fun," said Julia. "Where in heaven's name did he get that white chef's hat that he wore when we had church barbecues?"

"Too long a story," I said, holding my memories close.

Conversation continued over a seafood meal on the island before we headed home, with everyone still talking about how much Earle meant to them, all with fondness and caring.

⁓

By late August, I felt ready to complete the rest of the agreement. It was going to be a long journey. I drove to my cousin's house just outside of Dallas—a nine-hour drive—and stayed with him and his wife the first night. The next day, I was off to Arkansas.

My goal was to get to Jim's house on Bear Lake in eastern Arkansas before dark. He had offered his lake home as a place to stay. Jim had spoken at Earle's memorial service, had been a great fishing buddy and colleague, and most importantly, he knew where H Lake was. All I knew was that it was somewhere in the White River National Wildlife Reserve.

Jim and his wife, Dorothy, were kind, gracious, and loving and welcomed me as well as the others. Mark and Michelle were able to come, as Memphis was only a four-hour drive away. They negotiated time off from work and got to Jim's house by late afternoon. The last to join us were Larry and his wife, Elaine. Larry had also been a long-time fishing buddy, racquetball competitor, and colleague of Earle's. They went way back. We gathered together that night around a long table set up in the cabin's living room, to enjoy a huge pot of chili that Dorothy had prepared, as well as salad, bread, and lots of red wine. Earle would have loved the spread.

Around that dinner, we celebrated my husband with love and humor. I was so grateful that Mark and Michelle were there to see their dad through others' eyes. Everyone told funny stories, as Earle's zest for life, as well as his quirks, invited much sharing.

"I'll never forget that time we all went to that conference out in California," said Larry, already trying to hold back laughter. "We checked in at the hotel and went to our room. And there comes Earle, with all kinds of things attached to him." He went on as we created this mental picture together. "He had a radio slung over one shoulder, this big black bag over the other shoulder, a large briefcase in his hand, and a Bowfit exercise trainer fastened across his back. Well, he couldn't get in the door. He just stood there, trying to figure it out."

Now Larry was bent over laughing at the memory, and we all laughed with him. Each of us could see it.

"I called him Gadget Man," said Larry, still laughing.

I thought, *what a wonderful name*. It fit.

I told about our trip to Alamogordo and the broken ankle. I spared no detail, including the Kentucky-blue cast, the big man zonked on pain killers, and me running out of gas on Interstate 10 across Texas. I included shouting at him, "Survive!" as I tossed a gallon of water at him, leaving to find a filling station. Mark and Michelle had not heard that one before. They sat there, eyes wide, trying to picture it. The stories went on for a while, all told with love.

The next morning, we set out in a caravan to mysterious H Lake. We rattled along country roads, getting deeper into heavy brush and taller trees. We passed a sign nailed to a tree with a white arrow: 'H Lake That Way.' The road soon after changed to dirt, with an increasing number of bumps and potholes. That went on for six miles, dust billowing out behind, and finally we stopped. There was the lake, identified as the one we were looking for. It was just a small, placid lake surrounded by a thick growth of trees and bushes. I had imagined it to be something a little more glorious. It was very quiet. I stepped out of the car with my pink zippered bag and walked down to the water's edge.

"Here are the ashes. Please take as much as you like, if you'd like," I said. "Earle just asked for his ashes to be spread out over the water, but you can add anything you'd like to that."

Everyone moved apart after taking ashes from the plastic bag. Michelle walked down a boat ramp. Mark walked a little farther up the shoreline. The rest of us lined up along the water's edge, offering ashes to the deep-green lake. It was quiet and lovely. I took a lot of pictures there and later gave everyone copies. Earle, probably without knowing it, had found a way for the people he loved to find closure in places he loved and felt nourished by.

Afterward, I treated everyone to lunch in a little country corner store at the juncture of two paved roads. It was great fun. The bait shop was in the front of the store. Fishing licenses were sold at a back counter, and the walls were lined with shelves full of flour, Crisco, kerosene lamps, flashlights, peanut butter, Velveeta, Spam, Ro-Tel, beans, jelly, crackers, jerky, assorted knives and fishing flies, and a whole variety of other sundries that might make a fishing trip complete. The aroma of cooking hamburgers and french fries filled the store. The kitchen was just off behind the cash register. We all ordered burgers because that was the only menu item. They were served with Bell jars of unsweetened or sweetened iced tea.

The party continued until everyone seemed to be talked out. Finally, it came time to say goodbye. We hugged, shared a few more laughs and tears, and then went separate ways.

I started out for northwestern Arkansas and the Buffalo National River that afternoon and got as far as Russellville where I spent the night. The next day I drove north to a town I remembered, called Ponca. There was a canoe put-in site there that our canoe club had used as the start-off point for a paddle from Ponca to Pruitt. Getting there meant driving several miles over bumpy dirt roads. I was alone for this part of the trip. It was too far for anyone else to come. I finally stopped at a site that allowed easy access to the river. The Buffalo was quiet here and the river slow-moving. I looked around. No one else was there. I suspected there was some sort of law about dumping human remains in national rivers. I stooped down with my pink zippered bag.

I suddenly remembered something I'd read a long time ago, in which the author refers to our physical body as the sandal for our soul. The sandal may become tattered and worn and scuffed, and may even lose a strap or buckle, but until the leather is totally worn away it provides protection for what is within. When it has finally outlived its usefulness, it falls away, leaving free that which it has protected.

"Earle, I am here at the river you loved," I said out loud. "I have done all that you asked, and now I'm done."

I emptied the whole bag of ashes into the river at once, close to the shore but far enough away for the water to move around, slowly easing them into the current. I watched as they became part of the mud, vegetation, and water, a cloud that hung there for a moment as if reflecting the clouds above, and then it was gone. With the melting of his ashes into the current, I felt a melting within. His spirit and my spirit, both finally free.

My mother died one year after Earle, almost to the day. She was eighty-nine. I have always felt that she waited in order to help me through that first year. I could call her anytime.

"Mom, I'm feeling such pain today. This is so hard."

"Yes," she'd say. "I know." And I knew that she did.

At the end, she had been in hospice care for six months, living in the nursing facility at Luthercrest. Her failing heart took her there. She was fully aware of her situation, and the hospice staff grew to love her. She was alert, engaging, and conversant until a week before she died.

The call came from the hospice nurse saying it was time for me to come. Mom had had a stroke.

Jane and I stayed in her apartment, which was still held in her name. Sometimes we sat with her together and at other times we spelled each other.

"Why don't we play these?" I said one afternoon. "I don't know who brought the CD, but I know she loves these old German hymns."

"I think that would be good," Jane said. "Even though she's not responsive, she might still be able to hear."

We closed the door to her room and sat there with her as we listened to the old familiar hymns, remembered from our childhood We had no way of knowing if she heard but, for me, the room became a sacred place. There was a presence, a deep peace. It seemed other loving beings were suddenly in attendance—my father, her brothers and sisters, her parents. We were there, with her, for a long time.

Other family started to come, and those who could not called. We held the receiver to her ear as grandchildren said goodbye.

"Jane, her breathing is starting to change," I said.

"I'll call the nurse."

The hospice nurse came in, a quiet, caring presence.

"The morphine drops will help ease her," she said. "And we can bring her up into more of a sitting position. That will help ease her breathing as well."

Jane sat on one side of the bed. I was on the other. We each took one of her hands and sat with her until she breathed her last. A blessed release.

CHAPTER 13

EPILOGUE

Nine years have passed. I live in Sedona, a place of beauty that I once shared with Earle. This is the place of the sweat lodge. I am not sure this will be a permanent home, but it is important that I'm here now. My house backs up to national forestland, and I am enfolded by the natural world. It is very quiet, and I am able to see and hear the rhythm of nature, unspoiled. Deer, coyote, and javelina wander through my yard at will. I love the Gambel's quail, plentiful here. They travel in community, constantly involved in elaborate conversations. Rabbits, quail, chipmunks, and an occasional squirrel, as well as multiples of songbirds, enjoy the seeds I put out for them. A red-tail hawk finds that doves are a tasty breakfast. Nothing is hidden here. Each being is true to its own role.

What I find in this amazingly beautiful red rock country is perspective. One can see the progression of geological change in the layers of the rock formations. It took sixty million years for this beauty to be created as winds, water, and volcanic activity sculpted the land. Human and non-human alike are shaped by interacting with unpredictable forces. I have come to understand that permanence and equilibrium are not absolutes and that, like the rock, I am continually being shaped.

My journey with my husband included painful times but also times of joy and loving. It was always a dance between good and not so good, but above all, for me, it was about commitment and love. I believe there are no accidents. Earle and I found our way to each other. We ultimately created a partnership different from the one that movies and books and fairy tales describe. For both of us, it was about a fundamental love and trust that allowed us to sustain a relationship through circumstances that we would have never predicted.

We all stumble through life, looking for love, safety, and trust. We search, bump into people, bounce off, move on, and for those of us who are fortunate, we find the person who is still there for us through the nitty-gritty and hard work of what daily life is all about. I never doubted that Earle was that person as much as his illness allowed.

My husband led me into adventures I would never have sought out on my own: fishing, sailing, canoeing, motorcycle riding, and co-ed recreational soccer. He led me into and joined me in spiritual study, mentored me in professional growth, and taught me about the joy of laughter and fun. And I learned about eddies.

Hot and sweaty after miles of paddling along the Eleven Point in Missouri, I called to Earle that I needed a break.

"Look, let's pull in over there," he'd said, pointing to a sheltered and shady spot along the bank to our left.

We used the current of the river and the placement of our paddles to spin us smoothly into the place he singled out.

"This is called an eddy," he'd said.

"Oh," I said. "It's so calm and quiet."

"Yes, it's a place where the water is pushed back in toward the bank and circles around like a tiny whirlpool," he said. "You can use it to rest or to look out over the river and plot your course."

EPILOGUE

We sat easily in the pool, held in place by the swirl of the water. Low-hanging arms of trees and river plant life created deep and welcome shade. The water was dark green there, almost black. We were part of the river yet removed from its energy.

"What a lovely river," I said.

"Thought you'd like it."

He'd smiled and reached into the red cooler that nestled in the bottom of the Old Town, pulled out a chilled bottle of water and handed it to me, along with a peanut butter and jelly sandwich, then took the same for himself.

We sat for a while, quiet. I looked out at the river. The surface was smooth.

"Now, if there were rocks and fast current ahead, you could take time to think through how you would approach them," he said.

"You just read my mind."

We rested a while longer, enjoying the peace, then returned to the river. Just a couple of paddle strokes took us back into the current. It felt good to be moving again.

The image of that quiet resting place reemerges for me often. An eddy, a refuge that allows restoration, then a gathering of energy to deal with the currents ahead.

Earle was a force. Living with him challenged me daily, and I grew into the fullness of myself because of him. I could do no less. Both of us lived our paths and did not shirk the journey. We were a balance for each other.

The healing room was my sacred space. Everyone needs such a place, filled with those things that are personally meaningful. For me, there were candles, stones, crystals, paintings, books, music, birdsong, and light. Our non-human environment exists to support us. We are not separate from it but in communion with it.

During this journey, my need to judge and control was worn away, softened. As I let go of those patterns, I was humbled. We are all part of the same family. We all share in the emotions given to us to feel.

I found compassion for Earle and compassion for all those who struggle on their path in this life. All those who hurt and can't find their way to a better place. I learned to have compassion for myself and all I have endured; compassion as well as love for myself as a person who struggles; at one with all the other life forms on this planet who struggle to live their truth.

I carry Earle with me, in my heart. We shared over twenty-five years together. I know he is still with me in whatever place he inhabits now.

My tapestry is complete. The background is woven with colors of calm and gentleness, the browns, greens, and blues of the earth and sky and plant life. Earle and I are woven, in the places where we appear, with the brilliant colors of the rainbow, as we were beings of passion and love and feeling. Surrounding us in the tapestry, like a strong, tightly woven web, are our children, our family, our friends, our loving communities, who dance the dance of life and love and caring with us, hands and arms linked. Peering out from hidden places, are birds and animals, spirit beings keeping their watch. Woven through all of this are strands of gold. They are my spirit threads, part of the whole, providing strength and endurance, reflecting the small pilot light that lives in each of us as a promise given for healing, compassion, wholeness, and love.

NOTES

1. Bowen, J. (1999). "Health Promotion in the New Millennium." *OT Practice, 4* (12), 14-18.

2. Rumi. (2004). *The Essential Rumi.* (C. Barks, Trans.) New York: Harper Collins.

ACKNOWLEDGMENTS

I am grateful for all of the staff at Sunbury Press, my new writing home for guiding me into the world of the traditional publisher. Senior Editor Jennifer Cappello patiently and gently led me into a cleaner version of my original text, which has greatly enhanced readability. Crystal Devine has fashioned a lovely interior design that enhances my words. Much appreciation to Lawrence Knorr who was the guiding hand in developing the cover design.

I want to thank kn literary arts, my point of entry into the journey of this book. Their quick response to my initial question as to whether I might have something worth developing led them to match me with my editor, author Carolyn Flynn at The Story Catalyst. Carolyn led me from my starting point—a fifty-five-page journal—into a book that I could have never imagined on my own. She pushed me always to look deeper, cheered me on in moments of doubt, and was a teacher of the craft of writing through her feedback, questions, and sage advice. I am forever grateful for her passion for story and for her friendship.

Laura Collins was editor of *OT Practice* for the American Occupational Therapy Association when I first met her many, many years ago. As a hopeful therapist eager to write, I showed her some of my work, and although she could not use my material then, she was most encouraging, telling

Acknowledgments

me to keep writing. Her words meant a great deal, then and now. And I cannot say enough for Jan Epton Seale, a gifted poet and writer, who during my years in Texas offered ongoing workshops for those interested in writing. Her gentle but clear voice supported all of us, men and women, who became the Texas Rio Writers, and my friends. In this environment of support and caring I was able to hear the beauty reflected in poem, memoir, essay, and mystery, told in the distinct voices of the authors. I am so grateful to everyone in that group for helping me learn about storytelling at its finest, from the heart and from each person's truth.

A number of people agreed to be readers for at least one of the drafts, giving valuable feedback. I thank Linda Collevecchio, PhD, for her helpful and astute comments about content and structure, for the final version of the title, for the image of the pilot light, and above all for her friendship and support. Additional readers Jan, Julia, Sally, Mary, Katie, Jen, and Jane all offered commentary and feedback that allowed me to see places that needed more work or alteration, and so strengthened the final draft.

Two people, no longer here, are part of me always. My mother was my model for writing, always hopeful, never giving up. And my husband, Earle, was forever a loving support.

My community of women, Jan, Sally, and Julia, walked my journey with me, were my support in time of weakness, and reminded me of joy, laughter, and compassion.

Another community of women, Rita and Clara, support me now as we travel life paths together. They are always ready to talk, listen, and share, all without judgment.

My sister, Jane, although not always sure about my strange urge to write, was always there for me when the going got tough and was always a voice of reason. I thank her.

Mark and Michelle reflect the strength of their father. Their fine minds, sense of fun, and support through the years is so cherished. They came later into my life but will always be part of it.

The closest and wisest women in my life are my daughters, Mary and Katie. They are strong, bright, creative, and refresh and nourish me with their honesty and their love every single day. They are my heart.

About the Author

JUDITH ELIZABETH BOWEN's vision is supported by forty-two years as a registered occupational therapist and a period of practice as a Certified Healing Touch Practitioner, enriching her spiritual and analytical gifts as a healer. More than half of her professional life was spent in clinical practice in a wide variety of health care settings. The remainder was spent teaching in undergraduate and graduate programs. She has been published in professional journals, a textbook, and three anthologies, and has presented widely at national conferences and workshops. She has also been recognized as a Fellow in The American Occupational Therapy Association for her achievements.

A native of Pennsylvania she now devotes her time to writing, painting, family and friends.

Made in the USA
Middletown, DE
15 July 2024